WORKING
WOMEN
AND THEIR
FAMILIES

FAMILY STUDIES TEXT SERIES

Series Editor: RICHARD J. GELLES, *University of Rhode Island*
Series Associate Editor: ALEXA A. ALBERT, *University of Rhode Island*

This series of textbooks is designed to examine topics relevant to a broad view of family studies. The series is aimed primarily at undergraduate students of family sociology and family relations, among others. Individual volumes will be useful to students in psychology, home economics, counseling, human services, social work, and other related fields. Core texts in this series cover such subjects as theory and conceptual design, research methods, family history, cross-cultural perspectives, and life course analysis. Other texts will cover traditional topics, such as dating and mate selection, parenthood, divorce and remarriage, and family power. Topics that have been receiving more recent public attention will also be dealt with, including family violence, later life families, and fatherhood.

Because of their wide range and coverage Family Studies Texts can be used singly or collectively to supplement a standard text or to replace one. These books will be of interest to both students and professionals in a variety of disciplines.

Volumes in this series:

Jacqueline V. Lerner

WORKING WOMEN AND THEIR FAMILIES

FAMILY STUDIES TEXT SERIES **13**

SAGE Publications
International Educational and Professional Publisher
Thousand Oaks   London   New Delhi

For information address:

SAGE Publications, Inc.
2455 Teller Road
Thousand Oaks, California 91320

SAGE Publications Ltd.
6 Bonhill Street
London EC2A 4PU
United Kingdom

SAGE Publications India Pvt. Ltd.
M-32 Market
Greater Kailash I
New Delhi 110 048 India

Printed in the United States of America

Library of Congress Cataloging-in-Publication Data

Lerner, Jacqueline V.
    Working women and their families / Jacqueline V. Lerner.
        p. cm. —(Family studies text series ; v. 13)
    Includes bibliographical references and index.
    ISBN 0-8039-4209-5. — ISBN 0-8039-4210-9 (pbk.)
    1. Working mothers—United States. 2. Work and family—United States. I. Title. II. Series.
HQ759.48.L48 1994
306.87—dc20   93-35559
                                                   CIP

94 95 96 97 10 9 8 7 6 5 4 3 2 1

Sage Production Editor: Rebecca Holland

Contents

Acknowledgments

I want to express my appreciation to the following individuals who contributed in important ways to the completion of this book: L. Annette Abrams, Jennifer Bowman, Domini Castellino, Cheryl Cook, Nancy Galambos, Richard Gelles, Julia Simonds, and Francisco Villarruel. My work on this book was supported in part by grant #HD 23229 from the National Institute of Child Health and Human Development (NICHD).

Jacqueline V. Lerner
Michigan State University

Dedicated to my father—
you will always be in my memory.

CHAPTER
1

A View of the Issues

IMAGINE THIS SCENE if you will: A mother of a young toddler pulls up at a day-care center, day-care home, or baby-sitter's house. The toddler is distressed; she has not had a good night's sleep. She cries at her mother's attempts to soothe her before they enter, and the attempts fail. Her mother, already agitated and late for work, takes her in where she hands her over to a caregiver, quickly mumbles the difficulties of the morning, and hurries off to work. The mother feels guilty all day and the stresses of work compound her anxiety. Meanwhile, her daughter settles into the morning activities, takes a short nap, and has a peaceful and playful afternoon.

This scene most likely takes place in thousands of cities across the country every day, with millions of mothers and their children. It conveys to some people the picture of a selfish mother who is putting her own desires and the benefits of employment ahead of the welfare of her child. It summons up a picture, to some, of an unhappy toddler, deprived of a good night's sleep, forced to spend the day without her mother. What is to become of this child? Is the care she is receiving from her caregivers as good as her mother could provide? Is it unhealthy for an infant or young child to be cared for by people other than her mother?

These are questions that arise when the scene described above is brought to mind. The pressures on mothers today are further compounded by the political atmosphere that has forced us all to pay attention to "family values." American mothers have been pushed into the middle of a debate that seems to be searching for the true definition of motherhood. They are forced to compare themselves to their own mothers and to the memories of growing up in the ideal world of "Ozzie and Harriet," where mom was home to see to the proper upbringing of the children and to provide a stable base for the family. Some are torn between their own desires to be like the images of the mothers of yesterday and the realities of today's world, some do not want to duplicate the behaviors of their own mothers, and some are simply not sure what the best solutions are for their families.

With the exception of never-married mothers, the majority of mothers are in the paid labor force today. For never-married mothers, 51% are not in the labor force. This trend of an increasing majority of mothers in the paid labor force, although slowing down, will almost certainly continue into the next century. What cannot be said with certainty is that mothers are in the labor force for the same reasons.

What is a good mother? Staying home all day does fit the "traditional" view of motherhood, but it does not automatically make one a good mother. The definition of motherhood has been transformed over the last generation, yet mothers are functioning in a society that fails to recognize the transformation. There are few national supports for mothers in the form of maternity leave or day care, leaving each mother to solve the complex issues that surround the decision to be employed. Risking job status, negotiating time off, and finding quality day care are some of the issues that many women have to begin to deal with even before the birth of the first child.

The decision to be an employed mother is prompted by personal, financial, family, and situational factors. Some women are the sole providers for their families; some are employed for personal satisfaction. Whether or not a woman's employment is healthy for her or for her family depends on her own personal and social characteristics and the needs of her family. Just because her friends, relatives, and the popular press may think it is unhealthy for a mother of an infant to be employed does not mean it is the wrong decision for a particular woman.

Many women who were pushed into the labor force for purely financial reasons have come to enjoy the fulfillment, the contacts, and the pride that employment brings. Some mothers still have a choice—they may sacrifice the amenities that employment can bring because they feel strongly that they need to be home with the children. Others, who have no choice, are totally stressed by the combination of work and family.

The questions revolving around whether mothers of young children should be employed are complex. The toddler described at the beginning of this chapter is probably not going to be adversely affected by her mother's employment if the care she is receiving is of high quality, if her mother is satisfied with her employment and home situation, and if she receives consistent, affectionate, and sensitive caregiving from all of the adults who take care of her. She *is* likely to be adversely affected if the care she receives is not of high quality, if her mother's mood and interactions with her are negative when they are together, and if there is instability in her home situation. The fact that maternal employment among middle-class women was not the norm for many decades has led the public to voice concerns about the consequences it may have for children. This book is aimed at sorting out some of these complexities.

MATERNAL EMPLOYMENT TODAY

As college students, the chances that your mothers are employed are much higher than they were a generation ago. Unless you have much younger siblings, it is likely that over 75% of your mothers and the mothers of teenagers and older elementary school children are employed. The traditional "Father Knows Best" family in which Mom stays at home to spend her time shopping, housekeeping, and caring for children is no longer the norm. In fact, as of 1989, fewer than 7% of families were characterized by the two-parent model of husband as breadwinner and wife as homemaker (Braverman, 1989).

What has accounted for this change? Today, most mothers, single or married, typically combine the roles of mother, housekeeper, employee, and child-care provider. They share these duties to some extent with their husbands (if they are married), their children, and hired help. They are driven to the work force for several reasons—personal fulfillment, economic necessity,

Table 1.1 Labor Force Participation Rates for Wives, Husband Present, by Age of Youngest Children: 1975 to March 1991. (For civilian noninstitutional population, 16 years old and over.)

Presence and age of child	1975	1980	1985	Total 1988	1989	1990	1991
Wives, total	44.4	50.1	54.2	56.6	57.6	58.2	58.2
No children under 18	43.8	46.0	48.2	48.9	50.5	51.1	51.2
With children under 18	44.9	54.1	60.8	65.0	65.6	66.3	66.8
Under 6, total	36.7	45.1	53.4	57.1	57.4	58.9	59.9
Under 3	32.7	41.3	50.5	54.5	53.9	55.5	56.8
1 year or under	30.8	39.0	49.4	51.9	52.9	53.9	55.8
2 years	37.1	48.1	54.0	62.0	57.9	60.9	60.5
3 to 5 years	42.2	51.6	58.4	61.3	62.9	64.1	64.7
3 years	41.2	51.5	55.1	59.7	61.9	63.1	62.2
4 years	41.2	51.4	59.7	61.4	63.8	65.1	65.5
5 years	44.4	52.4	62.1	63.6	63.0	64.5	67.1
6 to 13 years	51.8	62.4	68.2	72.2	72.4	73.0	72.8
14 to 17 years	53.5	60.4	67.0	73.1	75.4	75.1	75.7

NOTE: Reprinted by permission of the U.S. Bureau of Labor Statistics, Bulletin 2340, and unpublished data.

boredom, or a combination. You may be surprised to learn that the majority of mothers will enter or return to the work force shortly after the birth of the first child.

The proportion of employed married women with children under age 6 increased from 18% to 30% between 1960 and 1970, and to 45% in 1980. In 1991 the rate was 59.9% (U.S. Bureau of Census, 1991). Table 1.1 details the increases in labor force participation for wives, with husband present, by age of the youngest child from 1975 through March, 1991 (U. S. Bureau of Labor Statistics, 1991).

Sandra Hofferth and Deborah Phillips (1987) project that by 1995, 70% of young children will have a mother in the labor force. This projection, based on current census data, is likely to be an underestimation. These percentages are higher for single women and for mothers of older children.

This increase in maternal employment during the last few decades has led mothers, fathers, caregivers, social scientists, and policymakers to be concerned about the consequences that a mother's work life and work conditions have on her children and her family life. After all, the roles traditionally ascribed to mothers are now shared with others—fathers are involving themselves more in child care and preschool programs are more common. Technology has cut down on the time one needs to spend on cooking and other housework; hence, mothers have more time on their hands than ever before.

The increase has also been associated with changes in forms of child care, and attitudes toward employed mothers. Infants, pre-schoolers, school-age children, and adolescents of the 1990s are experiencing the challenges, opportunities, and problems associated with life in families in which the mothers are wage earners. Psychologist Sandra Scarr (1984) has called attention to the idea that along with the benefits of mothers' employment, the management of work and family may place stresses on families and the solutions are rarely simple. How all of these changes are affecting children is at the forefront of empirical scrutiny.

Fortunately, there has been a burgeoning of research by child and family development specialists directed toward a common goal: to provide answers that will enlighten social scientists, social policymakers, and citizens about the influence that a mother's employment has on children and family. This book will examine the questions that have been asked and the answers that have emerged from these efforts, such as: What are the social, personal, and intellectual outcomes for children when their mothers are employed? It will concentrate on issues relevant to employed mothers and their families.

ISSUES IN MATERNAL EMPLOYMENT ACROSS CHILD DEVELOPMENT

During infancy and the preschool years, the one major issue for the family of the working mother is finding child care for the child or children. In many cases, this involves the placement of infants and preschoolers into day-care settings. Other types of care for infants and preschoolers are private, in-home care or family day care, where the child is taken care of in the home of another woman, usually with her children or other children present. In the 1980s, approximately 2 million children in the United States attended day care and an additional 5 million were in kindergarten (Santrock, 1989). The effect that alternative care (the care of children by someone other than their mothers) has on infants and preschoolers has become a major research question and is surrounded by controversy. Some of the questions that are being researched are: What are the effects of day care on the mother/infant and mother/child relationship? How does the day-care experience influence the infant or child's socioemotional development? What is the relationship between the quality of day care and the child's development? A discussion of the difficulties of finding high-quality day care for children is presented in Chapter 2.

Other issues involve the family. For example, does the father's role change when the mother becomes employed? What effect might the mother's employment status have on the father/child relationship? What influences do work schedules, maternal fatigue, and maternal role strain have on the family? These issues are discussed in more detail in Chapter 2.

When the children in the family reach school age, the issues broaden. Concern centers around how the child spends the hours after school. The "latchkey child," as it is popularly known, conveys the picture of a child who carries a key, opens the door, and remains at home alone after school for some period of time. Although it is true that several million children in the United States between the ages of 5 and 13 spend some portion of their day unsupervised (O'Connell & Bachu, 1988), the percentages differ according to the mother's employment status, the age of the child, the family income, and race. So the picture of the latchkey child is a complex one. Social scientists prefer to call these children "self-care" children to get away from the negative connotations associated with the phrase *latchkey child*. Attention has been directed at sorting out the effects of self-care on the child's development.

The issue of self-care is also relevant during adolescence, and we will see that how a child spends these hours and the types of supervision are key factors in how development is affected. The influences of a mother's employment on the social, intellectual, and sex role development of the school-age child and adolescent are important concerns.

Another issue that emerges during the school-age years and in adolescence is that of children who are substantially involved in household labor and how this involvement may affect their development (Bartko & McHale, 1991). The father's role in household labor and child care increases somewhat when the mother is employed, but in many cases the children take on substantially more household tasks when their mother is employed. During adolescence, issues such as the influence of a mother's employment status on occupational and educational choices and the mother as a vocational role model also assume importance (Lerner & Hess, 1988).

MYTHS SURROUNDING
THE EMPLOYED MOTHER

Many present-day myths make the topic of maternal employment a controversial one. You can hardly pick up an issue of a woman's magazine without being confronted by articles addressing the problems of finding child care, ways to manage stress from multiple roles, the guilt induced from nonemployed friends and family, and the like.

The major myth that permeates many of these articles is that mothers, because of their biological ties to their children, are instinctively the only ones who should be responsible for the primary care of their children. According to this myth, delegating care of the children to others who are not the mothers is unnatural, unhealthy, and risky for the child's development.

What is interesting about this myth is that it only became popular at the end of the 19th century. For example, in France in the late 18th century, infants of all classes were sent to wet nurses, sometimes as many as 100 or more miles away from home, for 3 to 5 years. Mothering as a full-time job did not exist. Not until the beginning of industrialization, when the birthrate for the white middle class in both England and the United States began to

Table 1.2   Present-Day Myths About Employed Mothers

1. Mothers, because of their biological ties to their children, are the optimal caregivers for their children.
2. Women are not able to effectively combine the roles of employee, mother, and spouse without harming family life.
3. Children will develop optimally if they receive their primary care from their mothers.
4. Day care or alternative care poses a risk to healthy child development.
5. A woman's place is in the home.

decline, did the role of the mother became central in the rearing of children.

Other myths and stereotypes are ones that cast doubts on the ability of women to be in the professional world— myths that place limitations on opportunities for woman to succeed. For example, the ideas that women cannot invest the time and energy necessary to be successful at the work place because of family demands, that women cannot be given the responsibilities that men can be given—these ideas are translated into actions that have created enormous barriers for women who desire or need to combine work and family. Assuming that a stay-at-home mother is a good mother is another myth that needs to be evaluated more closely. As early as 1962, Marion Yarrow and her colleagues investigated the parenting skills of stay-at-home and employed mothers. They were also interested in the mother's satisfaction with her role, employed or not. They found that the mothers who were rated lowest on positive parenting were those who were dissatisfied *and* at home (Yarrow, Scott, deLeeuw, & Heinig, 1962). Therefore, one cannot assume that because a child stays home with the mother that the child is receiving optimal care. Dispelling some of these myths has been a focus of current social science efforts. Table 1.2 outlines the major myths regarding employed mothers that are present today.

The most discouraging part of the pervasiveness of myths and stereotypes regarding women, mothers, and family roles is that they have guided the attitudes, ideas, and behaviors of many people who play a role in American children's lives—from the president down to the family next door. Since the 1970s a large body of research has accumulated to show that a woman's place is not necessarily in the home and that she can maintain other roles without compromising the stability of the family or the development of her children. In the next chapters some of these myths and the research that tries to dispel them will be explored.

Although this book is on the influences of the mother's employment, a section on father's employment is also included. After all, a child's development depends on both mothers and fathers. In the last decades research centered on how a mother's work changes family life and influences child development; recently, research has also begun to evaluate the influence that the father's job experiences have on the child.

Throughout this book there will be an emphasis on the idea advanced by psychologist Lois Hoffman (1979) that the link between maternal employment and child development is not a direct one. Over the past two decades studies have been able to determine that maternal employment per se does not seem to play a strong role in child development (Hoffman, 1979, 1980, 1984; Zaslow, Rabinovich, & Suwalsky, 1991; Lerner & Galambos, 1986, 1988). Increasing attention has been paid to the intervening factors that seem to influence the relationship between maternal employment and child development. These factors include child characteristics (e.g., involving gender, age, and temperament), family characteristics (e.g., socioeconomic status and culture, maternal role satisfaction, and father involvement), and characteristics such as the mother's employment circumstances and the quality of child care. Another factor that has been shown to influence the link between maternal employment and child outcomes is that of mother/child interaction; that is, researchers have documented that a mother's employment and variables associated with her employment affect the quality of the interactions that she has with her child. For example, a mother's role satisfaction influences the mother/child interaction, which in turn influences the child's development (Lerner & Galambos, 1986, 1988).

In sum, this book attempts to communicate to college students what is known about the links between maternal work, families, and child development. Many of the important conceptual and empirical issues are brought to the fore in an attempt to understand

the complicated lives of today's families. Only by an examination
of research findings can the myths that surround employed mothers and their families be sorted out from the facts.

Because the nature of the maternal employment/child and family development link is a complex one, it should be studied using
a perspective that lends itself to the complex nature of this link.
The life span developmental perspective and its assumptions can
help researchers examine the ways in which maternal employment affects the lives and development of children and families.

LIFE SPAN DEVELOPMENTAL PERSPECTIVE

The life span developmental perspective is a useful orientation
to approach the relevant literature on maternal employment primarily because, first, it provides a framework that allows us to
conceptualize the processes underlying individual and child development; and second, it suggests methodological approaches
for investigating developmental phenomena (Baltes, 1979; Baltes,
Reese, & Lipsitt, 1980; Baltes, Reese, & Nesselroade, 1977; Brim
& Kagan, 1980; Featherman, 1983; Nesselroade & Baltes, 1979;
Thompson & Lamb, 1986). The current state of research and theory
on maternal employment needs a perspective that can integrate
and organize streams of thought that are presently being discussed by professionals in the maternal employment field.

The life span developmental perspective has several major
assumptions. First, development is viewed as a lifelong process
with no particular segment of the life span assuming primary importance for the occurrence of all or most developmental processes.

A second assumption of the life span orientation is that there
are multiple determinants of development. For example, normative age-graded influences such as leaving school or getting married
exert an impact on the development of individuals at roughly the
same ages. History-graded influences help to determine development through their impact on individuals at specific points in
time (Baltes, Reese, & Lipsitt, 1980). For example, World War II
as a historical event had lasting impact on the development of

individuals who experienced it (Elder, 1975, 1981). One might also consider the experiences of women who enter adulthood during the current wave of female labor-force participation versus those who were young at the turn of the century (Huston-Stein & Higgins-Trenk, 1978). Third, non-normative life events such as death or divorce sometimes dramatically alter the life paths that the individual follows (Baltes, Reese, & Lipsitt, 1980). The assumption of multiple determinants of development leads to another aspect of the life span perspective—that of multidirectionality. With the numerous influences on development operating throughout the life span, there are multiple directions that development might follow (Baltes, Reese, & Lipsitt, 1980).

The assumptions of the life span perspective are compatible with a developmental contextual model. This model proposes that (a) the active individual and the active context are continually changing; (b) changes on one level of analysis promote changes in others; for example, a change in the sociocultural context will produce changes at the individual level, and vice versa; and (c) there is a potential for plasticity; that is, intraindividual change and interindividual differences in such change (Baltes, Reese, & Lipsitt, 1980; Lerner & Busch-Rossnagel, 1981; Lerner, Hultsch, & Dixon, 1983). The major emphasis of the developmental contextual model is on the relations between the individual and its context. Bidirectional relations between the organism and its context are assumed to characterize development (Bell, 1968; Lerner & Busch-Rossnagel, 1981). As shall be seen, the influences of maternal employment do not have to be assumed to be unidirectional—with the effect going directly from maternal employment status to the child; rather, one must take into account the multitude and complexity of variables that may influence the mother/child relationship, and hence the child, independent of employment status.

The developmental contextual model adds to the life span perspective notions of connectedness among early developmental processes and later ones, connectedness among the many influences on development (e.g., normative age-graded influences interact with historical influences and non-normative life events), and connectedness among many levels of analysis including, for instance, the individual, the family, the school, the workplace, and the culture (Lerner & Busch-Rossnagel, 1981).

With the current focus in the maternal employment literature on the specification of mediating variables and examination of the processes underlying maternal employment and child outcomes—processes that occur over time (Bronfenbrenner & Crouter, 1982; Zaslow, Rabinovich, & Suwalsky, 1991)—the life span developmental perspective, with its associated methodologies and research designs, shows much promise as a relatively new way from which to approach the study of maternal employment. Unfortunately, much of the research that will be presented in the following chapters is not guided by the life span developmental perspective. Research that has not been sensitive to the other factors that may influence the maternal employment/child development link sometimes assume that this link is a direct one. It is clear today that this is not the case. In detailing the research, careful attention will be paid to the studies that have attempted to uncover the complexities of the maternal employment/child development relationship.

IMPLICATIONS OF THE LIFE SPAN APPROACH FOR MATERNAL EMPLOYMENT

The life span approach to infant and child development and maternal employment has several implications for characterizing and gaining a better understanding of the complex interrelationships that exist. The major implications are discussed here.

1. Maternal employment is only one variable in the child's context that has an impact on that child's development and experiences. The relationship between individual development and maternal employment must take into account other related variables, including father's support of the mother working outside of the home, type of occupation the mother has, available child care, and the quality of the parent/child relationship.

2. The influences of maternal employment are not unidirectional. To speak simply of the effects of maternal employment on the child negates the possibility that the child (a) has any influence on his or her own development (i.e., implies that the child is only a passive recipient of external forces), or (b) may influence aspects of his or her context, such as the mother's attitudes and willingness to work outside the home. Because a major emphasis of the developmental contextual model is on the reciprocal relations between the active child and the active context (Lerner, Spanier, & Belsky, 1982), maternal employment should be seen as interactive with many other variables including the child's own characteristics.

3. The relationship between individual development and maternal employment should be conceptualized and studied across time. As researchers have noted (e.g., Zaslow, Rabinovich, & Suwalsky, 1991), the effects of maternal employment may diminish as the child grows older; this possibility brings into focus a concern with investigating such factors as how long the mother has been employed, the time periods in the child's life that the mother has worked outside the home, and the frequency with which she has returned home or changed jobs (Bronfenbrenner & Crouter, 1982; Zaslow, Rabinovich, & Suwalsky, 1991).

4. Maternal employment must be viewed within a historical context. The emphasis on the relationship between the sociocultural context and individual development may change with history. The children of employed mothers now have entirely different experiences than children did 40 years ago when employed mothers were in the minority (Bronfenbrenner & Crouter, 1982; Lamb, 1982). Indeed, the changing context of parenting is a historical change that will presumably affect children. As fathers become more involved in child care, issues regarding employment that were previously thought to pertain only to mothers will become important for them. For example, when a father makes a decision to be the primary caregiver, factors such as job characteristics, contextual supports for the father, and paternal attitudes and values will have import for the child's development.

Research that incorporated all of the above life span issues into its design would indeed be a major, long-term endeavor. It is not realistic to believe that many researchers in this area would want to, or have the funds to, pursue such a project. However, there are ways to incorporate the concerns of the life span developmental perspective into future research on maternal employment influences. An impetus to this incorporation is that, in increasing numbers, scientists and policymakers are realizing that the experience of maternal employment is not the same for everyone (Crouter, Belsky, & Spanier, 1984). Researchers are slowly moving away from examining the influences of employment per se, and are considering other variables in the child's context, with an emphasis on variables that mediate between maternal employment status and child outcomes.

Thus, it seems that researchers are becoming sensitive to some of the concerns raised by the life span perspective; that is, the importance of the context, multidimensionality, and the need to focus on developmental processes. The following chapters will present the research findings on the influences of maternal employment on child and family development with these concerns in mind.

PLAN OF THIS BOOK

You may believe that the myths and controversies that surround maternal employment have been blown out of proportion. You may think that it is a waste of time to spend money on research that attempts to sort out the influences of maternal employment on children. Your beliefs are not totally unfounded. After all, as an American you may be aware that it was only in 1993, after the inauguration of President Clinton, that the United States developed a national parental leave policy. Until this policy was passed, our government had viewed the rise in maternal employment as haphazard and unnecessary, and had not been supportive of spending time, money, and effort to determine if it influences children. My hope is that after you read this book you will realize that maternal employment is here to stay, that it is a necessary part of the lives of most families, and that attention needs to be focused on how it influences families.

This book is organized topically. Chapter 2 presents an overview of the changing employment patterns of mothers and how these patterns have altered family life. It includes a discussion of the changing attitudes toward women and work and how these changing trends present problems for mothers, families, and society. Chapter 3 presents the issues and empirical data regarding the relationship between maternal employment and the child's cognitive or intellectual development. Chapter 4 focuses on the relationship between a mother's employment and the child's emotional, social, and personality development. Chapter 5 presents information regarding the relationship between maternal employment and the child's educational and vocational choices. In this chapter, the relationship between paternal employment and child development is also discussed. Chapter 6 presents a discussion of the implications that the increasing trends in maternal employment have for social policy. It discusses what American families have in terms of national support for employed mothers and what they do not have. It also offers suggestions for future research and policy.

SUMMARY

This chapter has introduced you to maternal employment as a normative part of the lives of today's families. It has outlined some of the issues, the myths, and the realities that go along with being an employed mother today. The issues that surround the employed mother and her family and the potential effects that her employment can have on her children can only be sorted out through research efforts aimed at objectively delineating the conditions under which maternal employment influences children. The life span perspective is one research perspective that can be useful in the field of maternal employment. As this chapter has detailed, this perspective can integrate the complexities that arise when one is attempting to clarify the influences of maternal employment on children.

REVIEW QUESTIONS

1. Make a list of several economic or social changes that may be responsible for the increase in woman's participation in the paid labor force.
2. What are some of the myths that are commonly held regarding maternal employment?
3. How do the concerns about child development and maternal employment change across the child's life?

SUGGESTED PROJECTS

1. Trace the incidence of maternal employment in your family. Did your mother work when you were a young child? Did your grandmother? What are the reasons your mother gives for either working or not working?
2. Interview several of your peers to determine whether they believe in any of the myths about maternal employment discussed in this chapter.

2

Mothers at Work: Changes and Challenges

TRENDS IN MATERNAL EMPLOYMENT

As WE REACH THE CLOSE of the 20th century, mothers in the paid labor force are the norm. During the 1940s, 1950s, and 1960s, older married women composed the largest proportion of married women entering the work force. With the 1960s a new pattern emerged; young married mothers of preschoolers or school-age children began to enter the paid labor force. By 1980 almost two thirds of women with children between 6 and 18 were employed. Even more striking than this, by 1991 almost 60% of married women with children under age 6 were employed (U.S. Bureau of Labor Statistics, 1991). Figures 2.1 and 2.2 illustrate the historical trends for both female labor force participation and maternal labor force participation.

Most women are employed to supplement the family income, to support themselves and their families, or to gain personal fulfillment. It is true that many families redefine their standards of living once they get accustomed to a second income, and often the mother's income is used to provide for the second car, the second home, better vacations, and better education for the children. However, Adele Gottfried's work (1991) has shown that even when a mother's income is used for "luxuries," the material resources that her salary can provide can influence child development in positive ways.

A mother's decision to be employed or not is based on economic, personal, social, psychological, and family variables that are different for each woman. The decision to be employed can be filled with uncertainty, guilt, and frustration, especially for the mother

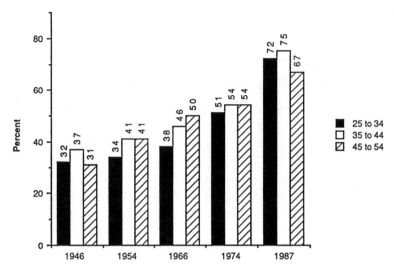

Figure 2.1. Historical Trends in Female Employment, 1946-1987 (by selected ages)
SOURCE: U.S. Bureau of Labor Statistics, Bulletin 2340

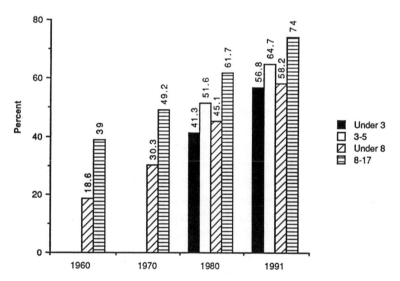

Figure 2.2. Historical Trends in Maternal Employment, 1960-1991 (Married women, spouse present, by age of children)
SOURCE: U.S. Bureau of Labor Statistics, Bulletin 2340, and unpublished data

of young children who needs to find high-quality, affordable child care. Social attitudes with respect to whether mothers of young children should be employed combined with economic uncertainty have left many mothers confused.

This chapter examines some of the changes and challenges that confront mothers who decide to enter the paid labor force. It looks at the changing social attitudes regarding women's paid labor, attitudes regarding whether children suffer when they are not cared for primarily by their mothers, and attitudes regarding women as individuals with desires to advance themselves in fulfilling ways outside the family. It then examines the many reasons that are responsible for women's entry or reentry into the paid labor force and discusses how some of these reasons evolved from social changes. Finally, it discusses the personal consequences that result from being an employed mother.

SOCIAL ATTITUDES TOWARD EMPLOYED MOTHERS

As women's roles have changed throughout history, so have ideas about whether mothers should be gainfully employed. When women had to work in the fields, there was not much worry about whether their children needed them at home. At the time of the Industrial Revolution, when men were employed away from home, a woman's place was viewed to be in the home with the children. Mothers were viewed as having primary responsibility for the home and the children, and the idea that mother's love was the best for children permeated society's view of the family.

At the end of the 19th century, scientific study about the developing child abounded. The early 1900s witnessed experts such as Arnold Gesell, John Watson, and Sigmund Freud who came forth to tell mothers how to provide optimal care for their children. The child was to be put ahead of all of a mother's own personal concerns and duties. The social attitude was one of "a woman's place is in the home with her child." Women who had desires to pursue higher education or careers were social misfits, especially if they had children. Society viewed these women with contempt, and the lack of research about the effects of maternal employment on children helped to embed these views further into social attitudes.

The attachment theories of Konrad Lorenz and John Bowlby solidified these attitudes. Attachment theories assert that there needs to be an early, continuous physical and emotional bond between mother and infant in order for the infant to develop optimally. The idea that mothers and their infants needed immediate and sustained physical contact in order to form the most optimal relationship with each other was prompted by the research of Konrad Lorenz (1965). In his animal studies he showed that animals need to "bond" to their mothers rapidly after birth in order for optimal development to occur. The "bonding" concept was expanded by Marshall Klaus and John Kennell (1976), who built on Lorenz's notion and informed the world that mothers who formed bonds with their infants in the first hours after birth were better mothers to them for years afterward (Scarr, 1984). Fathers and other caregivers had no place in this special relationship, and if maternal or child illness or hospital procedures prevented bonding, mothers felt guilty—they felt as if they would never be as attentive or caring as mothers who were able to bond with their infants.

Subsequent research on both nonhuman primates and humans has failed to find any sustained effects of early infant/mother contact on the mother/child relationship, particularly with regard to the mothers' attentiveness (Lamb, Frodi, Hwang, & Frodi, 1982; Svejda, Campos, & Emde, 1980). Yet, the belief that certain amounts of mother/infant separation will lead to less than optimal development is still held by some researchers (Belsky, 1986). Evidence has accumulated to show that infants may not develop optimally when they receive low-quality alternative care (Farber & Egeland, 1982). However, a point should be made here. Although data is not available to estimate how many infants are in low-quality care when their mothers are at work, it cannot be assumed that because the infant *does* stay home with a nonemployed mother that the infant is therefore receiving high-quality care.

The "attachment" concept of John Bowlby (1969) was similar to the bonding concept of Klaus and Kennell. He proposed that mother/infant attachment was necessary in order to provide the baby with a safe base from which he or she could explore the world and to provide an emotional haven for the regulation of anxiety and stress. Mary Ainsworth (1973) built on this idea and proposed that there were individual differences in the quality of mother/child relationships that were due to differences in the sensitivity of the mother to the baby's needs in the early months of life. According to Ainsworth, "secure" attachment results when mothers accurately read their babies' cries and respond quickly to them. These babies are able to form secure relationships with their mothers that set the stage for healthy development. On the other hand, "insecure" attachments are formed when mothers are slow to respond to their babies or cannot accurately read their signals. According to Bowlby and Ainsworth, insecurely attached infants are at risk for problems in development.

Subsequent research has again questioned the exclusiveness of the role of maternal sensitivity in promoting a secure attachment between mother and child (Lamb & Campos, 1983). Differences in infant temperamental characteristics, as well as genetic and contextual factors, can also set the stage for the quality of the mother/child relationship. Child developmentalist Jerome Kagan (1987) has argued that the power of the attachment bond in infancy is overdramatized and that infants are highly resilient and adaptive. Thus, they can stay on a positive developmental trajectory even when exposed to wide variations in parenting. Others have criticized attachment theory for ignoring the diversity of infants' contexts and experiences such as the increase in day care, mothers' employment, peer experiences, and cultural values. These factors have not been adequately considered in attachment theory (Lamb, 1988; Lamb, Thompson, Gardner, Charnov, & Estes, 1984).

As the above paragraph delineates, attachment theory and its related ideas have been scrutinized by child developmentalists in recent years. Even with a surge of solid research that has called into question the role of early mother/infant attachment in the child's development, the idea that mothers are doing irreversible harm to their babies if they return to work is prevalent in some circles.

Employment After World War II

The expanding economy after World War II opened up many job opportunities for women. But the view of maternal employment in the 1950s, 1960s, and 1970s was still negative and attachment theory supported this negative view. Research efforts such as those of psychologist Lois Hoffman (1974) were beginning to show that it was not necessarily detrimental for a mother of young children to be employed. In fact, some earlier research had already shown that a dissatisfied mother, employed or at home, was detrimental to her child's development (Yarrow, Scott, deLeeuw, & Heinig, 1962). The most frustrating finding for developmentalists was that maternal employment seemed to have few consistent effects on child development (Bronfenbrenner & Crouter, 1982; Lamb, 1982). This inconsistency has led social scientists to conclude that the experience of maternal employment is not the same for everyone. This conclusion has prompted a surge of research that looks at the different influences and mediating processes that are involved in the link between maternal employment and child development. This research will be the focus of chapters 3 through 6.

Today, the economic realities of employment, combined with research findings indicating that maternal employment is not universally detrimental for children, should put most mothers at ease. They do not. Societal attitudes regarding maternal employment have not caught up with the movement for equality between the sexes. Women still feel guilty if they must work, guilty if they desire to work, depressed if they have to go on welfare to support their children, and upset if they cannot afford high-quality child care. Society has never held the view that men should *not* attempt to combine career and family, yet it has scrutinized the combination of employment and motherhood. The view that a woman must do both (be a "supermom") has contributed to the strains that already exist when one combines work and family.

REASONS FOR WORKING

The two most common motives that have pushed women into the labor force are economic need and personal fulfillment, and most women would not leave their jobs even if economic pressures were reduced (DeChick, 1988). It is true that families are likely to redefine their standard of living once the mother is employed, making economic need a relative concept. Divorce and separation have contributed to the rise in maternal employment, but they are not totally responsible for this increase. Married women who are employed full-time and year-round contribute two fifths of their family income.

There are many other reasons that can account for the increase in women's labor force participation. Married women are bearing fewer children, allowing for a quicker reentry into the labor force and an easier time in balancing employment and family roles. Women are also postponing the age at which they bear their first child, allowing them to obtain more education, which increases their opportunities for employment. Educational opportunities for women are increasing, and many women are delaying marriage and childbirth in order to pursue a career. The attitudes regarding women's capabilities in entering certain professions have changed somewhat as some women are rising to the top in managerial and executive positions. Increasing longevity has also contributed to women's desires to be employed; after her last child leaves home a woman can have a decade or more to be employed before retirement.

In sum, women who choose to combine work and motherhood are in a paradoxical situation. On the one hand, there are more job, educational, and career opportunities than ever before. Changes in family size, household conveniences, and labor-saving devices have contributed to an increase in free time. On the other hand, the employed mother is faced with multiple roles that still remain primarily her responsibility, with negative attitudes from family members and society, and with the lack of a truly supportive set of social policies such as parental leave and day-care support.

CONSEQUENCES OF COMBINING WORK
AND MOTHERHOOD

In addition to the guilt that the employed mother experiences, there are numerous other consequences that arise from the combination of work and motherhood. Women in general, regardless of whether they are mothers, face tremendous occupational barriers in spite of the advances they have made in education and in the labor force. In addition, their role strain (the strain that results from carrying out multiple roles) is likely to be higher than for women who are not employed, and they face the difficult task of finding high-quality, affordable child care. Some of these consequences are discussed in more detail below.

Occupational Barriers

The majority of women continue to be channeled into traditionally female low-paying, low-prestige jobs with little influence (Fox & Hesse-Biber, 1984). If they are fortunate enough to be in prestigious careers they are often not taken seriously, not afforded the same opportunities for advancement as men, and not paid equally for the same work. This situation adds to their role strain, because they often have to work harder to "prove" themselves.

An additional barrier that women face is that the workplace has remained relatively inflexible to the needs of both men and women who both work and are responsible for raising a family (Silverstein, 1991). Inflexible work hours, the limited parental leave policies, and the lack of child-care support policies all contribute to the strain of managing both work and family. Because women are still bearing the primary responsibility for both the care of the children and the management of the household, these barriers contribute more to the strain on mothers than on fathers (Hochschild, 1989; Scarr, Phillips, & McCartney, 1989). Although research efforts have continued to try to sort out the consequences that a mother's employment has on her children, similar efforts to evaluate the negative consequences that the lack of societal supports has on both mothers and families have not been launched (Silverstein, 1991). Chapter 6 presents a more detailed discussion of the lack of national, social, and occupational supports for employed mothers.

Role Strain

In terms of role strain, women's family roles impose enormous demands that may limit their occupational time and contribute to their stress and strain. On the other side of the coin, employment roles and demands likewise detract from the time available for family, and therefore can also contribute to role strain. Men's household work participation has not increased along with women's rise in the labor force, leaving many employed women faced with taking care of the household responsibilities when they get home. This second set of responsibilities, appropriately termed the "second shift" by Arlie Hochschild, is the major reason that employed women, especially those with children, are experiencing strain (Hochschild, 1989; Scarr, Phillips, & McCartney, 1989). Needless to say, this leaves little or no time for rest, leisure, or evening activities devoted to job advancement. When demands and expectations cannot be met, frustration, guilt, and role strain increase, which has implications for the mother's mental health as well as the well-being of her children (Lerner & Galambos, 1988).

In addition, research has found that mothers are particularly stressed when there is a lack of support from their spouses in attitudes toward their employment and a lack of participation by their spouses in child care and household work (Anderson-Kulman & Paludi, 1986; Pleck, 1985). The strain associated with mothers' feelings that their husbands are not sharing the family responsibilities not only affects their stress levels, but it also has negative effects on wives' perceptions of their marriages. However, husbands do not seem to share similar perceptions (Gilbert, 1988; Pleck, 1985). This mismatch in perceptions can add additional stress to the marital relationship.

In spite of the data that show possible negative consequences of maternal employment on the marital relationship, overall there appears to be a positive balance for both husbands and wives in most dual-career families (Gilbert, 1985; Wortman, 1987). Even men who hold traditional values about employment and motherhood recognize the positive contribution a mother's salary can make to the family's income and standard of living. Of course, the satisfaction of both husbands and wives will depend on their gender role attitudes and on their abilities to manage their time, work, and family demands (Voydanoff & Kelly, 1984). Nancy Pistrang (1984) finds that for mothers in particular, satisfaction depends on how committed they were to their employment before they became mothers. In her research, mothers with high work commitments prior to the birth of their children who stayed home for 5 or more months after the birth reported greater irritability and depression, decreased marital intimacy, and lower self-esteem than mothers with low work commitments.

The multiple roles of employed mothers impinge different degrees of strain on them. Mothers are individuals, with different expectations, perceptions, attitudes, and values. These differences influence how the experience of employment will play a role in their development and in the development of their children.

Finding Child Care

Child-care support and parental leaves have not been adequately addressed at the national level; therefore, each individual family is left to tackle their needs to be employed and to find high-quality care for their children. High-quality care, especially for infants, is scarce and very expensive. This leaves the disadvantaged and minority populations of women, the ones who are employed out of true economic necessity, in the worst possible situation. If they want to stay off welfare they must be employed, usually in low-paying jobs, and they cannot afford high-quality child care. This can increase their guilt, their role strain, and may ultimately have negative influences on their children.

In 1988 there were 19.7 million women in the United States labor force with children under 15 (O'Connell & Bachu, 1988). This translates into 30.3 million children with employed mothers, of which 9.5 million were under age 5 and 20.8 million children were 5 to 14 years old. There are many different child-care arrangements that families use; the choices are made by families based on cost, convenience, and of course, quality. Even when arrangements are

Table 2.1   Primary Child Care Arrangements Used by Employed
Mothers for Children Under 15 Years: Fall 1988

Type of arrangement	All children (percent)	Children under 5 years (percent)	Children 5 to 14 years (percent)
Total	100.0	100.0	100.0
Care in child's home	17.0	28.2	11.9
By father	9.6	15.1	7.1
By grandparent	2.5	5.6	1.1
By other relative	2.2	2.2	2.2
By nonrelative	2.7	5.3	1.5
Care in another home	14.3	36.8	4.0
By grandparent	3.5	8.2	1.4
By other relative	2.1	5.0	0.7
By nonrelative	8.7	23.6	1.9
Organized child care facilities	9.8	25.8	2.5
Day/group care center	6.4	16.6	1.7
Nursery/preschool	3.5	9.2	0.8
School-based activity	1.2	0.2	1.7
Kindergarten/grade school	52.3	1.3	75.5
Child cares for self	1.6	0.1	2.3
Mother cares for child at work[1]	3.8	7.6	2.1

NOTE: [1]Includes women working at home or away from home.
SOURCE: M. O'Connell & A. Bachu, Who's minding the kids? U.S. Department of
Commerce, *Current Population Reports*, Fall 1988.

made, mothers experience many failures in these arrangements
that cause them to miss work. Caregivers may become ill, the
child may become ill and therefore not able to attend day care, or
caregivers may decide to quit on short notice. Tables 2.1 and 2.2
detail the percent of children in different types of care during the
fall of 1988 and the percent of parents who reported having lost
time from work due to a failure in child-care arrangements
(O'Connell & Bachu, 1988).

As mentioned earlier, the task of finding child care, especially
for infants and preschoolers, is difficult. Infants and preschoolers
need intense supervision, in a high-quality, nurturing environment. There are not enough organized, licensed, high-quality centers available for all of the children who need care. Even if there
were enough centers, quality care for young children is the most

Table 2.2   Time Lost From Work Due to Failures in Child Care
              Arrangements: Fall 1988

Marital status, type of work shift, and employment status of the woman	Women only (percent)	Wife and husband (percent)	Husband only (percent)
MARRIED, HUSBAND PRESENT			
Total	3.7	0.6	0.7
Day shift	3.9	0.7	0.8
Employed full time	3.7	0.9	0.9
Employed part time	4.5	0.2	0.6
Not a day shift	3.5	0.3	0.6
Employed full time	3.5	0.7	0.6
Employed part time	3.5	0.1	0.6
ALL OTHER MARITAL STATUSES[1]			
Total	4.4	(X)	(X)
Day Shift	4.5	(X)	(X)
Employed full time	4.6	(X)	(X)
Employed part time	4.4	(X)	(X)
Not a day shift	4.2	(X)	(X)
Employed full time	4.5	(X)	(X)
Employed part time	3.8	(X)	(X)

NOTES: X Not applicable
[1]Includes married, husband absent (including separated), widowed, divorced, and never-married women.
SOURCE: M. O'Connell & A. Bachu, Who's minding the kids? U.S. Department of Commerce, *Current Population Reports*, Fall 1988.

expensive care. Families with children in some type of child-care arrangement spent between 5% and 21% of their monthly income on child care in 1988 (O'Connell & Bachu, 1988). Figures 2.3 and 2.4 show the average weekly cost of child care for various income groups and the percent of monthly family income spent on care during the fall of 1988.

As you can see in Figure 2.3, families with higher incomes spend more per week on child care. Because high-quality care is the most expensive, middle-income and upper middle income families will be the most likely to have their children in quality care. This weighs the possible negative influences of low-quality care on the side of the children from the lower income groups. Mothers in these lower income groups most likely realize that their children are receiving less than optimal care. The frustration and

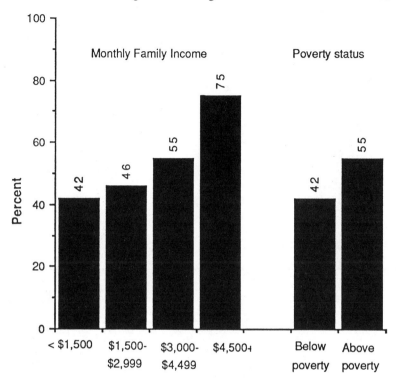

Figure 2.3. Average Weekly Cost of Child Care, Fall 1988
SOURCE: M. O'Connell & A. Bachu, Who's minding the kids? U.S. Department of
Commerce. *Current Population Reports*, Fall 1988.

guilt that may follow from this realization can lead to an increase
in stress for the mother, negative mother/child interactions, and
less than optimal job performance.

Work/Family Spillover

You may recall from your childhood that occasionally your
father came home from work complaining that he had "a bad day
at the office." The problems and stresses of the day at work may
have affected his mood, his interactions with you and your siblings,
or his interactions with your mother. At another level, they may
also have affected his health and psychological well-being. In
addition, family problems may have distracted him at his office,

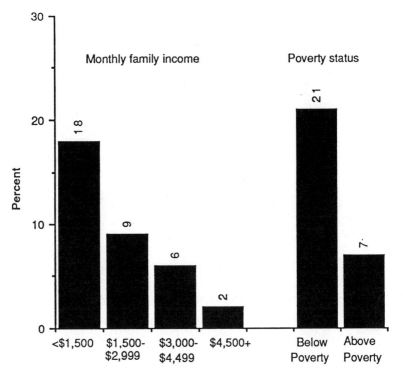

Figure 2.4. Percent of Monthly Family Income Spent on Child Care: Fall 1988
SOURCE: M. O'Connell & A. Bachu, Who's minding the kids? U.S. Department of Commerce, *Current Population Reports*, Fall 1988.

decreased his concentration, or lowered his productivity. This is what psychologists and sociologists have termed "spillover"— when the demands and stresses from one arena (job or family) get carried over into the other. There can be both positive and negative spillover. Positive spillover occurs when the satisfaction and stimulation from one arena spread into the other. Negative spillover occurs when problems and stresses in one arena make it difficult for the person to adequately perform in the other. Several researchers have studied this phenomenon in both men and women (Piotrkowski, 1979; Crouter, 1984; Emmons, Biernat, Tiedje, Lang, & Wortman, 1990). Most of the research concentrates on the spillover from work to family; Ann Crouter's (1984) work, on the other hand, has concentrated on spillover from family to work.

In her research on spillover from work to family with lower middle income men, Chaya Piotrkowski (1979) found that workers who liked their jobs and had some control over their job demands were more available at a psychological level to their families when at home. As you would expect, the opposite occurred in men with extremely stressful jobs—they brought their work tensions home and were either unavailable or withdrew from family interaction. In general, the job characteristics that create stresses are heavy work loads, role ambiguity, health and safety hazards, job insecurity, role conflicts, pressures for quality work, and the underutilization of abilities.

Aside from job demands and characteristics, an individual's orientation to work can also spill over into family life. High levels of job involvement among male professionals and managers have been found to be related to high levels of work/family conflict (Mortimer, 1980; Voydanoff, 1982). These studies also found that job involvement was related to lower levels of marital satisfaction. However, in the study by Jeylan Mortimer (1980), the link between job involvement and marital satisfaction was moderated by spousal support; that is, when wives supported the occupational involvement of their husbands, this involvement did not seem to be associated with lowered levels of marital satisfaction.

In terms of job satisfaction, sociologist Patricia Voydanoff (1982) found that in a national sample of male professionals and managers, high levels of job satisfaction were associated with high levels of marital and family satisfaction and lower levels of work/family conflict. Similarly, in a sample of middle to upper middle income mothers, role satisfaction was associated with more positive mother/child interaction patterns (Lerner & Galambos, 1985).

The notion that family life has an effect on the work setting is also relevant here. This type of spillover, from family to work, has not been as well studied as spillover from work to family. Women and men alike do not leave their family life on the doorstep before they begin their workday. The effort by some companies to provide supports to families in the form of flexible schedules or child care is testimony to the fact that family issues may affect workers' performance, commitment, and satisfaction (Crouter & Garbarino, 1982). From the previous discussions about women continuing to take on primary responsibility for the home and children even when they are employed, it is probably no surprise that spillover from family to work is higher among mothers of small children.

In a sample of lower middle income men and women, Crouter (1984) found that the extent of the spillover from family life to work depends on the individual's role as a family member. In her sample, women with children under 12 were more likely to feel a negative impact of the family on work life because family responsibilities sometimes resulted in absenteeism, tardiness, and inefficiency. In addition, they reported that they hesitated to take on new responsibilities at work because of family demands. This pattern was not present in women with older children, implying that the employed mother of young children is "at risk" for negative spillover from family to work.

In a study of professional women, Carol-Ann Emmons and her colleagues (Emmons, Biernat, Tiedje, Lang, & Wortman, 1990) found that the majority of women felt that their family lives had positive or neutral effects on their careers, and that their work lives had positive effects on their marital relationships. They reported that their husbands were supportive of their careers, and that they were relatively satisfied with the contributions that their husbands made to household work and child care. However, many of these women reported that they felt that their careers had negative effects on their relationships with their children. Because these women still assumed primary responsibility for the daily management tasks of the household and children, there was little time left for "quality" activities with the children. Although research has found that employed women do spend as much time in quality activities with their children as nonemployed mothers do, the professional women in this sample did not perceive this to be the case.

This discussion further supports the notion that the experience of maternal employment is not the same for everyone—not for every mother, child, or family. Researchers need to concentrate on the individual differences in mothers, children, and families when

examining the link between maternal employment and c
development.

SUMMARY

The trends for mothers entering or returning to the work force
are continuing, and the next decades will clearly show that employment for the mothers of young children is the norm. Maternal
employment is here to stay, although the reasons for working vary.
Although social attitudes regarding maternal employment are
not as negative as they were several decades ago, attitudes have
not caught up with the reality of combining work and family. Many
mothers are feeling guilty, stressed, and apprehensive about their
multiple roles. Researchers must be committed to studying the
impact that maternal employment has on mothers and families.
The dilemma that faces the employed mother in America is real
and complex. From the research presented in this chapter, it seems
that employed mothers from differing economic groups are deal-
ing with the balancing of multiple roles. These roles appear to
have consequences for their own mental health, their relationships
with their husbands, and their relationships with their children.
This chapter has attempted to outline some of the attitudes, social
changes, and experiences that define maternal employment today. The next chapters will explore the question that is a major
focus of this book: What is the relationship between maternal
employment and child development?

REVIEW QUESTIONS

1. What are the various trends that describe maternal employment
   over the last few decades?
2. What is the concept of "attachment"? How has it influenced societal attitudes concerning maternal employment?
3. What are the various reasons given for maternal employment?
4. What are some of the contributors to role strain in employed mothers?

SUGGESTED PROJECTS

1. Use United States census data to show the increases in labor force participation among women from 1900 until today. Are the trends different for black women?

2. Make a chart showing how much time most mothers of young children spend in their various roles of housekeeper, child-care provider, cook, chauffeur, spouse, community volunteer, and friend. Now add to this chart full-time employment. Are there enough hours in the day for a woman to fulfill all of these roles?

CHAPTER

3

Maternal Employment and Children's Intellectual Development

CHILDREN'S SUCCESS IN SCHOOL and their overall intellectual development are primary concerns of all parents. From the early months of their children's lives, parents stimulate and teach their children both directly and indirectly. They take them shopping, point out objects, talk to them, and read to them—all activities that help young children learn about their world.

For the most part, it is not necessary for young children to be enrolled in early education programs in order to learn what they need to in the early years of their development. In a warm, supportive, and stimulating environment, children are exposed to all of the necessary ingredients for healthy intellectual development to occur. The point here regarding a warm, supportive, and stimulating environment is not meant to imply that all children who stay at home with their mothers receive this kind of quality care. Certainly, with the rates of child abuse and neglect in this country, parental or mother care cannot be assumed to be quality care.

However, when mothers are employed, concerns are raised about the type of environment the child experiences. The following questions are typically asked: What happens when very young children spend a large proportion of their time outside their own home, without their mothers? Do they experience an environment that will allow their intellectual development to proceed on a healthy track? Do school-age children receive the homework supervision and attention they need to succeed in school when their mothers are employed?

During infancy, these concerns may stem from the idea that the lack of affordable infant care will undoubtedly leave the infant in an unstimulating environment. Certainly, the early research on maternal deprivation (Bowlby, 1951; Spitz, 1946) contributed to this view. With regard to child intellectual development, recent research has not been able to prove that maternal employment per se is linked to lowered intellectual and cognitive development in children. In fact, as chapters 1 and 2 describe, the link between maternal employment and child development is not a direct one. Factors related to the child, the family, and the child-care context can, and do, contribute to the child's development. During childhood and adolescence, concerns are raised as to whether maternal employment interferes with the supervision of the child after school, and whether the mother is still able to provide the necessary support for homework and other school-related activities.

Differences exist between the idea, on one hand, that there is a direct link between maternal employment and child development, and, on the other hand, that there are numerous mediating and moderating variables that play a role in how maternal employment may influence child development. If you take the view that there is a direct link between maternal employment and child development, then you believe that the mere fact that a mother is employed will influence her child's development. This view does not consider any other characteristics of the mother, child, or family, and assumes that maternal employment has a universal influence on children. Even though this view was held by some in past decades, it is not popular today. Researchers recognize the individual circumstances of maternal employment and the differences among individuals and families. Research findings have documented the inconsistencies that have led psychologists such as Lois Hoffman (1974) to assert that "the distance between an antecedent condition like maternal employment and a child characteristic is too great to be covered in a single leap" (p. 128). Now, researchers are in the midst of sorting out the intermediate steps or variables that are involved. These steps involve both mediating and moderating variables. According to Richardson and colleagues (Richardson, Dwyer, McGuigan, Hansen, Dent,

Johnson, Sussman, Brannon, & Flay, 1989), moderating variables may affect the direction and/or strength of the relationship between two variables. These moderators may help us to understand under what conditions maternal employment is related to child development. Socioeconomic status is one such moderating variable, because the literature shows that maternal employment has different implications for children from different social classes. On the other hand, a mediating variable helps to describe the mechanism through which maternal employment is related to child outcomes. Using the same example of social class, looking at patterns of family interaction or gender role beliefs may help to determine why social class differences emerge.

This chapter will detail the research on the influence of maternal employment on the child's intellectual and cognitive development with an emphasis on those studies that have tried to analyze some of the moderating and mediating variables involved. Before this presentation of research, it is useful to review some of the methodological and conceptual shortcomings that limit the usefulness of these findings.

Limitations of Research

The most limiting aspect of many of the early studies on maternal employment influences is the fact that they lacked a guiding theory or framework within which results could be interpreted. This limitation has not totally disappeared from the research; some studies are still concerned only with delineating differences between children of employed versus nonemployed mothers. Studies that have gone beyond this "direct relationship" approach and have looked at the other mediating and moderating variables that play a role in the maternal employment/child development link are more conceptually driven and sophisticated. For example, recognizing the importance of the home context in the child's development, psychologists Allen and Adele Gottfried (1988) have carefully evaluated the characteristics of the home context in a longitudinal study of the relationship between maternal employment and child development. In addition, psychologist Lindsay Chase-Lansdale and her colleagues (Chase-Lansdale, Michael, &

Desai, 1991) have studied the maternal employment/child intellectual development link by evaluating some of the mediating variables that are involved. For example, they look at social class and cultural differences in their sample, as well as the mothers' patterns of employment.

Another limitation is that from study to study there are differences in how maternal employment is measured, in how the outcome variables (i.e., school achievement and social adjustment) are measured, and in the age of the child at the time that maternal employment status was assessed. In addition, many studies combine gender and social class, despite both gender and social class differences. Because these limitations make it difficult to compare studies, it is not surprising that there are so many inconsistencies in the literature. These limitations should be kept in mind when examining the literature on the relationship between maternal employment and the child's intellectual and academic functioning.

COGNITIVE AND INTELLECTUAL DEVELOPMENT DURING INFANCY AND EARLY CHILDHOOD

Research that has focused specifically on the influences of maternal employment on infant cognitive and intellectual development is surprisingly scarce. More attention has been paid to the influences on infant social and emotional development and parent/infant attachment. The few studies that have been done present mixed results. For example, using the Bayley Scales of Infant Development, Ellen Hock (1980) and Frank Pedersen and his colleagues (Pedersen, Cain, Zaslow, and Anderson, 1982) found no differences in the cognitive development of infants from employed and nonemployed mother families. Another study (Schacter, 1981) found no differences in language development between infants of employed and nonemployed mothers, but did find differences in Stanford-Binet intelligence scores—infants with nonemployed mothers scored higher. Other research has evaluated the cognitive development in a sample of toddlers whose mothers returned to work during early infancy and found no differences in problem-solving ability between these toddlers and toddlers whose mothers resumed work later on in the child's infancy (Goldberg & Easterbrooks, 1988). A more extensive longitudinal study of the influences of maternal employment on the home environment and children's development by Allen and Adele Gottfried (1988) found no direct relationship between the mother's employment and cognitive or intellectual development during infancy or toddlerhood.

In their longitudinal study of maternal employment from infancy through the school years in a predominantly white, middle-class sample of children, the Gottfrieds (1988) found absolutely no indicators that maternal employment was related to social or intellectual problems in the child. Their study was very comprehensive in that they obtained repeated measurements of child characteristics from infancy through age 7 and they also assessed numerous characteristics of the home and of the parents. Their study is exemplary in that it attempted to sort out the complexity of variables that affect child development whether or not the mother is employed.

What is interesting about the Gottfrieds' work is that they were unable to replicate a finding that had come up fairly consistently in the literature—that maternal employment seemed to be related to lowered intellectual ratings for middle-class sons. Their findings demonstrate that there are other characteristics that play a role in the child's development whether or not the mother is employed. For example, in their sample, the employed mothers held higher educational attitudes for their children, and these attitudes were related to higher levels of cognitive development, academic achievement, and social development. So, even when a finding appears to have some consistency, one has to evaluate other factors before attempting to generalize findings across groups.

Other research that does not focus on the effects of employment per se has shed some light on the link between maternal separation and infant cognitive development. This research looks at the influences of maternal separation when disadvantaged babies are placed in enrichment programs and investigates how these programs affect the infant's cognitive development. Although this research is not specifically examining the influences of maternal employment on these infants, mothers are separated from their babies and, from this standpoint, the effects of maternal/infant separation on cognitive development can be learned. These studies have shown that high-quality early enrichment programs can, and do, improve children's intellectual development and school achievement (Brooks-Gunn, 1989; Burchinal, Lee, & Ramey, 1989; Clark-Stewart & Fein, 1983; Lazar, Darlington, Murray, Royce, & Snipper, 1982; Ramey & Campbell, 1987). The early childhood programs in these studies were of very high quality, so some have cautioned against assuming that any early childhood program will be beneficial. However, other research has shown that enrollment in child-care centers of varied quality can also positively influence toddlers' cognitive development (Burchinal, Lee, & Ramey, 1989; Golden, Rosenbluth, Grossi, Policare, Freeman, & Brownlee, 1978).

Thus, research has not been able to clearly link maternal employment to any lowered infant or toddler cognitive and intellectual indices. As the previous chapters have discussed, maternal employment is associated with many factors in the family and the broader environment. For example, maternal employment has different meanings in different cultures and different social classes, and in single- versus two-parent families. The influence that it will have on the child also depends on the mother's own intellectual level, attitudes, occupational aspirations, supports, and the father's level of support and participation in the family. Most of the studies to date have not taken into consideration the complexities of maternal employment and the mediating influences of these variables.

Another study that has addressed the complexity of the influences of maternal employment on the child's intellectual development is the research of Lindsay Chase-Lansdale, Robert Michael, and Sonalde Desai (1991). These researchers have used the sample of the National Longitudinal Survey of Youth (NLSY) to investigate the influence of maternal employment on children. This sample includes different cultures and social class groups and consists of approximately 12,000 people. Between 1986 and 1988, assessments were made on the cognitive and emotional development of the children of the women of the NLSY (approximately 5,000). Because detailed labor force participation information was collected on these women, this data set has been able to shed new light on the influences of maternal employment on the cognitive and intellectual development of children.

Chase-Lansdale, Michael, and Desai (1991) used the Peabody Picture Vocabulary Test-R (PPVT-R) to assess intellectual ability. The PPVT-R is a brief assessment of word knowledge or receptive vocabulary. It is highly related with other tests of IQ, but it is not considered to be an IQ test itself. The child is presented with four pictures per page, with each page becoming increasingly difficult. The child is then asked to point to the picture that best represents the word said by the examiner. The investigators were interested in determining the effects of various employment patterns, mother's earnings, family size, child spacing, race, marital history, mother's verbal ability and education, mother's age at the birth of the child, and the child's gender on cognitive development. Thus, this research is a much more thorough attempt at delineating the complexities of the maternal employment/child development relationship.

In terms of the race of the child, both black and Hispanic children performed more poorly on the PPVT-R at age four than did white children. It has been argued that the PPVT-R may be culturally biased (Sattler, 1974), so this finding should be interpreted with caution. The mother's verbal ability did significantly predict the child's ability, and the mothers' levels of education predicted verbal ability in boys but not girls. Whether the mother was a teenager or not was not predictive of PPVT-R scores, but this may have been because the researchers controlled for income level. Typically with young mothers, the age of the mother per se is not predictive of poor outcomes in the child, but rather the economic conditions that are usually worse with teenage mothers (Furstenberg, Brooks-Gunn, & Chase-Lansdale, 1989).

Additional analyses showed no effect of family income, mothers' earnings, or marital history on child performance. However, birth order was negatively related to performance for girls and child spacing was related to performance in boys (boys who had more widely spaced siblings performed better). This finding is in line with other research in child development suggesting that when children in large families are spaced close together, they do not have the chance to interact with adults (either parents or older siblings) frequently. They therefore show cognitive and intellectual deficits when compared to children in families in which the spacing between children is wider.

In terms of maternal employment patterns, neither the timing nor the patterns of the mother's employment had an influence on the PPVT-R scores for either boys or girls. Because there are several studies indicating that boys in middle-class families do not fare as well on measures of intellectual ability when their mothers are employed full-time, Chase-Lansdale and her colleagues sought to determine if this finding would hold up in the children of the NLSY. Urie Bronfenbrenner (1988) has argued that the reason that middle-class boys do not fare as well may be because in the higher income groups, maternal separation may have a more significant effect on the child, whereas in the lower income groups other variables may be more influential. That is, in the lower income groups, a mother's additional income may provide more stability and resources for the family and thus may counter any effects of maternal separation. However, in the middle- to upper-income brackets the mother's income does not really add significantly to the family's resources (i.e., it does not take the family above poverty level as it might in lower income families).

Thus, in higher income families maternal separation may have more of an impact. The results from the NLSY support this argument. Among middle-income families, when mothers were continuously employed, boys had significantly lower PPVT-R scores. This was not the case in the lower income group nor for girls of any income group. Intermittent employment by the mother was not related to boys' performances in any income group. This finding supports some existing research that seems to indicate a certain vulnerability of boys in the middle class when their mothers are continuously employed from infancy.

Bronfenbrenner, Alvarez, and Henderson (1984) have tried to interpret why in some studies middle-class boys do not fare as well as girls or lower-class boys. They found that when parents were asked to describe their children, the least favorable descriptions were from full-time employed mothers describing their sons. The most positive descriptions were of sons when described by part-time employed mothers.

A recent investigation by Ellen Greenberger and Robin O'Neil (1992) set out to determine if the descriptions of children by parents that Bronfenbrenner and his associates (1984) found would still hold today. They failed to replicate the key finding of Bronfenbrenner, Alvarez, and Henderson (1984), that part-time employment was linked to more positive maternal descriptions of sons. They found that maternal employment was more strongly linked to fathers' and teachers' perceptions of children. Fathers perceived their 5- to 6-year-old children as having more problem behaviors when mothers were currently employed full-time. Both fathers and teachers viewed children's behavior as more problematic when less educated mothers had been employed for long periods throughout the child's lifetime.

Greenberger and O'Neil (1992) made a point similar to the one made by the Gottfrieds (1988). The mothers and fathers studied by Greenberger and O'Neil were both more educated and better off financially than were the mothers and fathers studied by Bronfenbrenner and his associates (1984). These parents may have had more resources to help them with effective parenting and in the balancing of their multiple roles. It is possible that part-time employment no longer holds the rewards that it did years ago, and that the mothers with more education and thus more gratifying jobs were more satisfied. In past research, maternal satisfaction has been linked to more positive perceptions of one's child (Alvarez, 1985). Thus the historical context within which maternal employment occurs as well as other characteristics of the mother, father, and family must be examined.

In spite of the research that calls into question the negative influence of maternal employment on middle-class sons, Bronfenbrenner (1988) has asserted, and Chase-Lansdale, Michael, and Desai (1991) have argued, that when mothers are absent in middle-class families, considerable interactions and stimulation may be lost and are not replaced in the child-care setting. In the lower income families, the loss of the mother's presence is replaced by amenities that her income can provide—amenities that seem to cancel the negative effect of her absence.

This finding runs counter to the results of the study by the Gottfrieds (1988) in which they found no intellectual problems for boys of employed mothers. However, the Gottfrieds looked at the mother's educational attitudes and aspirations for her children, whereas some other studies do not. This inconsistency in the research findings further illustrates the need to look at a comprehensive picture of the context of maternal employment before conclusions can be drawn.

Some researchers who accept the negative findings for middle-class boys have tried to explain why this finding then holds for boys but not for girls. Research has begun to indicate that parents believe that their daughters are more vulnerable than their sons, and may therefore provide deliberate protection from the stress that maternal employment may bring to the family (Zaslow & Hayes, 1986). In addition, older observational studies in middle-class families in which the mother is employed have revealed that mothers overcompensate for their absence with their daughters but not with their sons (Stuckey, McGhee, & Bell, 1982; Zaslow, Pedersen, Suwalsky, Cain, Anderson, & Fival, 1985). Other reasons may be that boys are more irritating to parents and may receive more negative interactions from them; in addition, boys may be more vulnerable in the child-care setting than girls, to whom caregivers generally respond more favorably.

It should be noted here that the quality of the alternative care for these children has not been assessed. Other research by Ross Thompson (1991) has shown that the quality of the infant care is of vital importance to the child's development. In the literature that has examined infants, toddlers, and preschoolers, the only finding seems to be one that links continuous, full-time maternal employment with lowered cognitive performance in middle-class sons, and this finding cannot be unequivocally accepted. The next section will detail the research on school-age children and evaluate what other variables seem to be important for older children.

COGNITIVE AND INTELLECTUAL DEVELOPMENT IN SCHOOL-AGE CHILDREN

Examining the relationship between maternal employment and the school-age child's cognitive and intellectual development has been a major focus of much of the literature over the last several decades. As discussed earlier, most of the studies done in the 1960s yielded conflicting results, with children of employed mothers sometimes faring better than their nonemployed counterparts, and sometimes faring worse. In addition to the lack of consistent findings, many of these studies did not analyze their data to look for social class or gender differences. Other variables that have since been found to play a role in the influence of maternal employment on child development (i.e., mother's education, career commitment, pattern and timing of employment, full-time versus part-time employment, and attitudes) were also not considered.

Studies in the 1970s and 1980s began to sort out some of the complexities of the influence of maternal employment on school-age boys and girls. There were not always clear-cut results, and many inconsistencies were still emerging. The effects for daughters seem to be both more clear and more positive than for sons, especially in the area of cognitive development. Although no studies found that daughters of employed mothers invariably performed better academically than daughters of nonemployed mothers, there has been evidence of an increased career orientation in these daughters (Banducci, 1967; Below, 1972; Smith, 1969).

The pattern of findings for middle-class sons is less consistent. As discussed above, some studies that have examined the effects of maternal employment in lower-class versus middle-class sons have found that mothers' working outside the home is associated with lower academic achievement for sons (Banducci, 1967; Brown, 1970; Gold & Andres, 1978a, 1978b). Other studies have failed to replicate this finding (Gottfried & Gottfried, 1988; Lerner & Galambos, 1988). Lerner and Galambos (1988) found no negative associations between maternal employment during the son's early years and their cognitive and intellectual development either concurrently or later on in their sample of middle-class children. They did find, however, that when mothers were more satisfied, whether or not they were employed, they had more positive interactions with their children. The children of satisfied mothers tended to be rated as better adjusted than the children of dissatisfied mothers.

Some studies have also favored the interpretation that maternal employment is detrimental to middle-class sons when the mother has been employed continuously and full-time during the child's preschool years. As mentioned previously, Chase-Lansdale, Michael, and Desai (1991) found this to be the case in the children of the NLSY, and an earlier study by Delores Gold and David Andres (1978b) paralleled this finding.

However, this finding should not be generalized too broadly. Other work (Gottfried & Gottfried, 1988; Lerner & Galambos, 1988) has shown that maternal employment had no negative relationship with sons' achievement or cognitive development. Many other factors can be operating that could cancel out the risks or contribute to better performance.

For example, middle-class employed mothers who have high levels of education compensate for the time spent away from the child (Hoffman, 1980). Thus, the mother's education, her role strain, and her satisfaction will affect her willingness and ability to compensate for the time lost with her child. Moreover, Lois Hoffman (1984) has warned against comparing the children of employed versus nonemployed mothers. Because of smaller family sizes, labor-saving devices, and other technology that has freed up enormous amounts of time typically spent in running a household, the employed mother of today probably spends as much time with her children as the nonemployed mother of yesterday.

In line with this notion, Martha Moorehouse (1991) has found in a sample of first graders that there were no differences in the children of employed versus nonemployed mothers in terms of the children's school competence. This finding held for those children who experienced frequent shared activities with their mothers. Thus, children whose mothers made an effort to spend time with their children in activities, whether they were employed or not, had the highest levels of school competence.

In any event, the research findings have documented that at the very least, the experience of maternal employment is not the same for every family nor for every child. Children within the same family can have different experiences because of their ages, their genders, and their interactions with their mothers and fathers. What a family will experience when a mother is employed depends as well on the social class of the family, their attitudes about employment and childrearing, and the amount of benefits or strains that are placed on the family as a result. These factors should be kept in mind when reviewing the research that has examined these influences of maternal employment on the cognitive and intellectual development of adolescents.

COGNITIVE AND INTELLECTUAL DEVELOPMENT IN ADOLESCENTS

The developmental needs of adolescents are quite different from those of infants, toddlers, or school-age children. Although they still need the love, attention, and guidance of parents, adolescents have increasing needs for autonomy and independence. Perhaps that is why research efforts that have been directed at examining the relationship between maternal employment and adolescent development are not as abundant as research with younger children. That is not to say that no research exists—it does. Most of the better studies have been done in the last decade, and much of it is related to the issues of adolescent self-care, parent/ adolescent relationships, gender role development, occupational attitudes, and academic functioning. This section will consider any research that is relevant to the experience of maternal employment on adolescents and how that experience may influence their cognitive and intellectual development.

Lois Hoffman (1979) has argued that a mother's experience of maternal employment may be more positive when her child is an adolescent because of the decreasing child-care demands and the increasing independence of the adolescent. Therefore, the employed mother of an adolescent child may be a more satisfied mother because she will not experience the decreased need for her mothering in quite the same way as a nonemployed mother. In fact, employment may serve to make her much freer to encourage independence in her child, thus having a positive influence on the child's development. In fact, it has been reported that as adolescents advance in age, their mothers tend to detach from them, and report high levels of satisfaction when they are involved in activities independent of their adolescents (Montemayor & Brownlee, 1982).

The previous discussion of the effects on younger children has shown that there are many variables that will be potential moderators of the influences of a mother's employment on her child. This pertains to adolescents as well. Gender differences continue to emerge in the studies of adolescents, with daughters again showing higher levels of achievement when their mothers are employed (Query & Kuruvilla, 1975; Rees & Palmer, 1970). Middle-class adolescent sons in some studies show the same trend as in the younger samples: lowered achievement for the sons of employed mothers (Banducci, 1967; Gold & Andres, 1978b). Other studies find no differences in adjustment or achievement in sons of employed versus nonemployed mothers (Burchinal, 1963; D'Amico, Haurin, & Mott, 1983; Lerner & Galambos, 1988; Rosenthal & Hansen, 1981).

Much of the interest in whether the adolescent child's academic performance suffers when his or her mother is employed is based on the premise that employed mothers do not have sufficient time to supervise their children's homework and academic pursuits. The research addressing this premise has again shown that there are no consistent influences of maternal employment on the adolescent child. For example, it has been found that it is not maternal employment that is related to the child's academic competence, but the mother's educational attainment and aspirations for her child (Hutner, 1972). Similarly, other researchers have found that when mothers hold professional jobs, they spend more time in reading activity with their children and have more plans for the child's education (Jones, Lundsteen, & Michael, 1967; Frankel, 1964). Maternal employment in these studies had no direct relationship to the competence of these children.

More recent research has found that a more important influence on the adolescent's competence is whether or not the mother is satisfied with her role. For example, a high level of maternal role satisfaction was related to a higher grade point average in the adolescent regardless of the mother's employment status (Lerner, Hess, & Tubman, 1986).

The idea that variables such as maternal role satisfaction or role difficulty would have more of an impact on the child's development than maternal employment per se is not a new one. In 1962, Marian Yarrow, Phyllis Scott, Louise deLeeuw, and Christine Heinig found that if mothers were in their preferred roles they showed no differences in childrearing; hence, it was role satisfaction, rather than work status, that contributed to positive interactions with their children. In addition, in 1963 Lois Hoffman reported differences on maternal, child, and teacher measures when comparing satisfied and dissatisfied employed mothers. She found that satisfied mothers who were employed were perceived by their children as showing more positive affect and less severe discipline. In contrast, dissatisfied mothers perceived their children as more argumentative, and teachers reported them as displaying assertive and sometimes hostile behavior in the classroom.

In both elementary school children and adolescents, research findings show that congruence between the mother's attitude and her employment status (i.e., role satisfaction) led to positive child outcomes in both social adjustment and school performance (Baruch, 1972; Gold & Andres, 1978b; Pearlman, 1980; Williamson, 1970; Woods, 1972; Lerner & Galambos, 1985, 1988). Hence, the question of how maternal employment status may directly influence the child may be invalid—research needs to go beyond maternal employment status and examine the "processes" by which maternal employment influences children.

In an attempt to gain an understanding about which processes could be involved in the relationship between maternal role satisfaction and child development, Lerner and Galambos (1985) hypothesized that if a mother is more satisfied with her role, then this should influence her interaction with her children. They hypothesized that higher levels of satisfaction would be associated with more positive mother/child interaction, and more positive mother/child interaction would be associated with better child adjustment. Their hypothesis was supported, thus indicating that mother/child interaction may be one process by which child development is influenced by maternal role satisfaction. This process model will be detailed in the next chapter.

Maternal Work History

By the time a child reaches adolescence, his or her mother's employment patterns could have been characterized in a number of different ways. She could have been continuously employed full- or part-time, intermittently employed full- or part-time, or nonemployed. In addition, the pattern could have been one of increasing or decreasing employment since the child's birth. In any event, looking at how a mother's concurrent employment affects child functioning masks any effects that past employment history may have on later child functioning. As mentioned previously, some researchers have found that certain patterns of employment are associated with certain outcomes in the child. For example, Chase-Lansdale, Michael, and Desai (1991) have reported that continuous, early employment from infancy was associated with lowered PPVT-R scores in a sample of middle-class boys. Thus, researchers need to look at the mother's employment history and not simply whether she is employed at the time the outcome variable is measured.

In many studies, children have been grouped together based on mothers' work status without consideration of the time, onset, or duration of mothers' employment (Hetherington, Camara, & Featherman, 1983). Evaluating maternal work history provides a more dynamic view of how work history, timing, patterns, and transitions between employment categories may be related to child functioning. The studies that have examined maternal work history are not plentiful; the few that have been done with adolescent school achievement or intellectual development as an outcome are presented below.

Delores Gold and David Andres (1978b) compared the achievement of 10-year-old children of mothers who had been working uninterrupted since the children were between 2 and 4 years old with the children of mothers who had not worked after their children's births. In this study, there were no differences between middle-class daughters of employed versus nonemployed mothers. For sons, however, Gold and Andres found a similar pattern that has been observed among younger children; that is, middle-class boys of employed mothers scored lower on language and mathematics achievement tests than middle-class boys with nonemployed mothers, middle-class daughters with employed or nonemployed mothers, or working-class daughters of nonemployed mothers.

In another study, Gold and Andres (1978a) were not able to replicate these findings. They compared the achievement of 14- to 16-year-olds whose mothers who had been full-time homemakers for the majority of the children's lives with the achievement of adolescents whose mothers had worked full-time for at least 4 consecutive years. They failed to find significant differences between the nonemployed and employed groups for sons or daughters in either the middle or working class. In trying to reconcile these findings with the other Gold and Andres study, one hypothesis is that the negative effects of maternal employment are less pronounced when the mother begins work later in the child's life (in the study of 14- to 16-year-olds, most mothers began work when their children were about 7). Another hypothesis, supported by the research of Chase-Lansdale, Michael, and Desai (1991), is that the most negative effects for boys seem to occur when the mother is employed continuously from early in the child's life, as shown in the Gold and Andres (1978b) study with 10-year-olds.

Research with older adolescents (high school students) has similarly led to contradictory interpretations. In an analysis of the High School and Beyond (HSB) survey of a national sample of 2,720 sophomores and seniors, a cumulative negative effect of the mother's employment over the child's lifetime was reported (Milne, Myers, Rosenthal, & Ginsburg, 1986). This finding has been criticized because Milne and his colleagues deleted subjects with incomplete information, so the analysis was biased toward the higher socioeconomic groups and therefore the negative effects of maternal employment may have been overestimated.

In addition, it could be argued that the negative effects found by Milne, Myers, Rosenthal, & Ginsburg (1986) were attributed to the students whose mothers were employed during the preschool years. This does not mean that this finding supports the idea of a "critical period" for the impact of maternal employment. The subjects in this sample were preschoolers 20 years ago and therefore one could interpret this as a historical effect.

Another study of interest used HSB data to evaluate the influence of the mother's movement in and out of the work force by looking at patterns of employment. The adolescents whose mothers reported increasing or stable part-time employment patterns had the best school achievement records; the worst records were of adolescents whose mothers reported decreasing or fluctuating employment patterns (Heyns & Catsambis, 1986). Perhaps the instability of the mother's work schedule produced stress in the families of the latter group.

The research on the link between maternal employment and adolescent achievement indicates that employment may have a slight negative influence on middle-class sons, as has been found in some younger samples. However, this effect is influenced by the mother's role satisfaction and her employment history and patterns. Hence, the complicated picture of maternal employment influences is once again evident.

SUMMARY

This chapter has attempted to sort out the research that has provided information on the relationship between maternal employment and child intellectual functioning. The picture is complicated. Most researchers would agree that maternal employment is associated with either neutral or positive developments for daughters. For sons, however, the picture is less clear. Some studies have found some negative relationships between intellectual functioning and maternal employment in sons in middle-class samples, and some have found no relationship. In the studies that found no relationship, factors such as maternal attitudes and family resources seem to play a role. These findings cannot be generalized to all children and it has become clear that family and contextual characteristics play an important role in the maternal employment/child development link. The next chapter will focus on the relationship between maternal employment and the social and personality adjustment of children.

REVIEW QUESTIONS

1. What are some of the major limitations of the research on maternal employment influences?
2. What is the most consistent trend in the research findings regarding maternal employment and child intellectual development?
3. What are some of the explanations that have been advanced to explain the link between maternal employment and lowered achievement in middle-class sons?
4. What are some of the "process" or "moderating" variables that are thought to play a role in the maternal employment/child development link?

SUGGESTED PROJECTS

1. Interview one or two families in which you know the mother is employed. Ask them about schedules and amount of time spent with the children. Try to get an idea of whether the mother is experiencing role strain.
2. Interview one elementary school child, one junior high school child, and one high school child whose mothers are employed. Ask them how they feel about their mothers' employment and their family situations since their mothers have been working. Try to determine if there are differences in their ideas and attitudes about maternal employment.

Maternal Employment and Children's Socioemotional Development

CHILDREN OF EMPLOYED MOTHERS are cared for in many different child-care arrangements. They may be cared for in their own homes by a relative or nonrelative, in a family day-care home in which one woman typically cares for her own children and other children, in a day-care center, or in a baby-sitter's home. As you may remember from Table 2.1, only 17% of children under 15 years old whose mothers are employed are cared for in their own homes. When considering only children under 5 years old, 28.2% are cared for in their own homes. Thus, the majority of children of employed mothers spend their day with other children and adults.

There has been much research attention paid to how this time spent without the mother might influence the development of the child's social and emotional relationships. Many child developmentalists, pediatricians, and parents see the relationship between the mother and child as primary, and maternal employment is seen as a potential disrupter of this relationship. You know from reading the previous chapters that *if* and *how* maternal employment disrupts the mother/child relationship is a complex issue.

At particular age levels, different variables can assume importance. For example, during infancy the influence of the day-care setting on the child's socioemotional development should be evaluated. During elementary school and adolescence, the child's after-school activities and level of supervision become important variables. This chapter will detail the research to date on the influence of maternal employment on the socioemotional development of children. Keep in mind that some of the limitations of research that were presented in chapter 3 will apply to the research presented in this chapter.

SOCIOEMOTIONAL DEVELOPMENT DURING INFANCY AND EARLY CHILDHOOD

The most significant amount of research on the influences of maternal employment on the socioemotional development of infants and young children is from research on day care, because most infants or preschoolers would not be in a day-care setting if their mothers were not employed. Thus, organized day-care centers that typically have 30 or more children are convenient sources for acquiring samples of children whose mothers are employed. There are problems with this type of sampling, however. First, only 24.4% of infants and young children whose mothers are employed attend day-care centers (O'Connell & Bachu, 1988). Because day-care centers have attracted the majority of the researchers, caution is needed in generalizing from conclusions drawn from these studies.

Another limitation of relying on day-care research is that other variables are, of course, influencing child outcomes. There is tremendous variability in the quality of care across day-care centers. The quality of the center care will influence the child, but in addition, the type of family that can afford and that chooses center care may be different from the type of family who cannot afford it or makes another choice. These family characteristics in and of themselves will influence the child. Thus, research findings from day-care studies cannot be generalized to all children of employed mothers. Nevertheless, because so much has been done with day-care samples it is important to critically evaluate this research.

You may be wondering what constitutes quality day care. There has been a considerable amount of attention paid to this question. The National Association for the Education of Young Children has published some guidelines to educate parents about what characteristics to look for in a day-care center or early childhood program. Table 4.1 lists these guidelines. To be licensed, day-care centers, day-care homes, and preschools must abide by state and federal guidelines regarding quality. The list on Table 4.1 incorporates many of these guidelines and additional items for parents to examine.

Mother/Infant Attachment

The question of how maternal employment influences infant socioemotional development turns to the issue of mother/infant attachment. This is perhaps the most controversial aspect concerning the infant/mother relationship. The concept of mother/ infant attachment was discussed in chapter 2.

As you recall, attachment theory and its related ideas are in the midst of controversy among child developmentalists. Even with a surge of solid research that has called into question the role of early mother/infant attachment in the child's development, the idea that mothers are doing irreversible harm to their babies if they return to work is prevalent in some circles.

Maternal employment and day-care research have become optimal arenas for the examination of the importance of early attachment on infant socioemotional development. Concerns have been raised regarding how day-care experiences affect the quality of infant/mother attachment and how differences in quality are related to infant socioemotional development.

Some researchers (e.g., Belsky, 1986; Belsky & Rovine, 1988) have concluded that extended day-care experience (i.e., more than 20 hours weekly) beginning early in life (i.e., within the first year) can be regarded as a "risk factor" for unhealthy infant/parent attachments. These findings have not been entirely consistent with those of other researchers (Clark-Stewart, 1989; Phillips, McCartney, Scarr, & Howes, 1987), who have argued that the conclusion that day care is psychologically detrimental to infants is premature and misleading.

Although researchers have documented that infants with substantial out-of-home day-care experiences sometimes behaved avoidantly and maintained greater distance from their mothers (Clark-Stewart & Fein, 1983), this finding does not hold across a wide range of studies (McCartney & Phillips, 1988). Researchers have also known that among preschoolers (Etaugh, 1980) the

Table 4.1 How to Choose a Good Early Childhood Program

Who will care for your child?
1. The adults enjoy and understand how young children learn and grow.
   Are the staff members friendly and considerate to each child?
   Do adult expectations vary appropriately for children of differing ages and interests?
   Do the staff members consider themselves to be professionals?
   Do they read or attend meetings to continue to learn more about how young children grow and develop?
   Do the staff work toward improving the equality of the program, obtaining better equipment, and making better use of the space?
2. The staff view themselves positively and therefore can continually foster children's emotional and social development.
   Do the staff help children feel good about themselves, their activities, and other people?
   Do the adults listen to children and talk with them?
   Are the adults gentle while being firm, consistent and yet flexible in their guidance of children?
   Do the staff members help children learn gradually how to consider other's rights and feelings, to take turns and share, yet also to stand up for personal rights when necessary?
   When children are angry or fearful are they helped to deal with their feelings constructively?
3. There are enough adults to work with a group and to care for the individual needs of children.
   Are infants in groups of no more than 8 children with at least 2 adults?
   Are 2- and 3-year-old children in groups of no more than 14 with at least 2 adults?
   Are 4- and 5-year-olds in groups of no more than 20 children with at least 2 adults?
4. All staff members work together cooperatively.
   Do the staff meet regularly to plan and evaluate the program?
   Are they willing to adjust the daily activities for children's individual needs and interests?
5. Staff observe and record each child's progress and development.
   Do the staff stress children's strengths and show pride in their accomplishments?
   Are records used to help parents' concerns about their child's development?

What program activities and equipment are offered?

1. The environment fosters the growth and development of young children working and playing together.
   Do the staff have realistic goals for children?
   Are activities balanced between vigorous outdoor play and quiet indoor play?
   Are children given opportunities to select activities of interest to them?
   Are children encouraged to work alone as well as in small groups?
   Are self-help skills such as dressing, toileting, resting, washing, and eating encouraged as children are ready?
   Are transition times approached as pleasant learning opportunities?

Table 4.1 Continued

2. A good center provides appropriate and sufficient equipment and play materials and makes them readily available.
   Is there large climbing equipment? Is there an ample supply of blocks of all sizes, wheel toys, balls, and dramatic play props to foster physical development as well as imaginative play?
   Are there ample tools and hands-on materials such as sand, clay, water, wood, and paint to stimulate creativity?
   Is there a variety of sturdy puzzles, construction sets, and other small manipulative items available to children?
   Are children's picture books age-appropriate, attractive, and of good literary quality?
   Are there plants, animals, or other natural science objects for children to care for or observe?
   Are there opportunities for music and movement experiences?
3. Children are helped to increase their language skills and to expand their understanding of the world.
   Do the children freely talk with each other and the adults?
   Do the adults provide positive language models in describing objects, feelings, and experiences?
   Do the staff plan for visitors or trips to broaden children's understandings through firsthand contacts with people and places?
   Are the children encouraged to solve their own problems, to think independently, and to respond to open-ended questions?

How do the staff relate to your family and the community?

1. A good program considers and supports the needs of the entire family.
   Are the parents welcome to observe, discuss policies, make suggestions, and participate in the work of the center?
   Do the staff members share with parents the highlights of their child's experiences?
   Are the staff alert to matters affecting any member of the family that may also affect the child?
   Do the staff respect families from varying cultures or backgrounds?
   Does the center have written policies about fees, hours, holidays, illnesses, and other considerations?
2. Staff in a good center are aware of and contribute to community resources.
   Do the staff share information about community recreational and learning opportunities with families?
   Do the staff refer family members to a suitable agency when the need arises?
   Are volunteers from the community encouraged to participate in the center's activities?
   Does the center collaborate with other professional groups to provide the best care possible for children in the community?

Are the facility and program designed to meet the varied demands of young children, their families, and the staff?

1. The health of children, staff, and parents is protected and promoted.
   Are the staff alert to the health and safety of each child and of themselves?

procedure—the "Strange Situation"—to assess the effects of day care on the infant/parent relationship. The Strange Situation is a 21-minute laboratory procedure (Ainsworth, Blehar, Waters, & Wall, 1978) that includes 3-minute episodes in which the mother is absent or the infant plays with an unfamiliar adult. The infant/mother reunion behavior is assessed by the infant's reaction to his or her mother's return. The infant is then characterized as either secure or insecure-avoidant, insecure-resistant, or insecure-disorganized. The insecure groups are thought to be at risk for later adverse developmental outcomes (Blanchard & Main, 1979; Belsky, 1984).

Reliance on only the Strange Situation as an assessment device, however, does not take into consideration other experiences the infant has had with strangers and separation or the temperamental characteristics of the infant (some babies are temperamentally difficult while interacting with their mothers in all situations). In addition, cross-cultural studies have shown higher rates of infants being assessed as insecure, especially in countries where babies have little experience with maternal separation as in Japan (see Lamb, Thompson, Gardner, & Charnov, 1985, for a review). Hence, researchers' attempts to link day-care experiences with the risk for insecure attachment or to link attachment classification with later adverse developmental outcomes must be examined warily.

The overall conclusions, in general, from reviews of day-care research are that there do not seem to be adverse effects for the mother/child relationship, that there are sometimes cognitive increases for children from disadvantaged backgrounds, and that children with day-care experience interact with their peers in more positive and in more negative ways (Hoffman, 1984). The issue that has become more relevant today is one of the quality of the care received at the center. In a study of public day-care effects in Bermuda (Schwartz, Scarr, Caparulo, Furrow, McCartney, Billington, Phillips, & Hindy, 1981) children with extensive care in centers where groups were large and where there were few adults per child showed significantly poorer adjustment on several cognitive and personality dimensions than children cared for at home or in home-based nonparental care.

Table 4.1 Continued

Are meals and snacks nutritious, varied, attractive, and served at appr time?

Do the staff wash hands with soap and water before handling food ar changing diapers? Are children's hands washed before eating ar toileting?

Are surfaces, equipment, and toys cleaned daily? Are they in good re

Are current medical records and emergency information maintained child and staff member? Is adequate sick leave provided for staff can remain home when they are ill?

Is at least one staff member trained in first aid? Does the center have consultant?

Is the building comfortably warm in cold weather? Are the rooms ve with fresh air daily?

2. The facility is safe for children and adults.

Are the building and grounds well-lighted and free of hazards?

Are furnishings, sinks, and toilets safely accessible to children?

Are toxic materials stored in a locked cabinet?

Are smoke detectors installed in appropriate locations?

Are indoor and outdoor surfaces cushioned with materials such as c wood chips in areas with climbers, slides, or swings?

Does every staff member know what to do in an emergency?

Are emergency numbers posted by the telephone?

3. The environment is spacious enough to accommodate a variety of a and equipment.

Are there at least 35 square feet of usable playroom floor space ind child and 75 square feet of play space outdoors per child?

Is there a place for each child's personal belongings such as a change of

Is there enough space so that adults can walk between sleeping childre

---

SOURCE: From "How to Choose a Good Early Childhood Program," by the Nationa tion for the Education of Young Children, 1990. Copyright 1990 by the National A for the Education of Young Children. Reprinted by permission.

day-care experience has been associated with a broader ra both negative *and* positive social behaviors.

The attempt to link these findings to infant/parent attac has exacerbated the concerns regarding the developme fects of early day-care experiences. Although attachment as a mechanism for evaluating the long-term consequences care is extremely controversial, research attention to the q has not diminished.

Another problem that adds to the controversy regard link between maternal employment, day-care experience, fant attachment is that many studies have relied on a

SOCIOEMOTIONAL DEVELOPMENT
IN PRESCHOOL CHILDREN

In terms of the social development of preschoolers, there is no compelling evidence that maternal employment is associated with differences in the types of interactions between employed versus nonemployed mothers and their children. It has been found that employed mothers who work more than 20 hours a week spend less time with their infants and preschool children than nonemployed mothers (Hoffman, 1989). However, this effect diminishes as the mother's level of education increases, and most studies have found no real differences in mother/child interaction between nonemployed and employed groups. In addition, some studies have shown that employed mothers are more highly interactive with their infants than nonemployed mothers, especially with respect to verbal stimulation (Hoffman, 1984; Zaslow, Pedersen, Suwalsky, Cain, & Fival, 1985).

Other studies that have evaluated the quality of the home environment of the preschool child in employed- and nonemployed-mother families have found no differences (Gottfried, Gottfried, & Bathurst, 1988; Mackinnon, Brody, & Stoneman, 1982; Owen & Cox, 1988). In studies on sex role development in preschool children, there is evidence that maternal employment is associated with more egalitarian sex role concepts for children whose mothers are employed (Gold & Andres, 1978a; Zaslow, 1987).

One aspect of parent/child interaction that seems to differ in employed versus nonemployed samples is that of independence training (Hoffman, 1979). Employed mothers seem to place a greater emphasis on independence training of their children. This difference proves to be an advantage for both the mother and the child because of the need for the child to establish independence from the mother as he or she moves through childhood. However, there are few consistent differences in the social development of preschoolers as a function of their mothers' employment status. When differences do emerge, it is difficult to evaluate whether the differences are attributable to maternal employment status or to some other variable in the context or the child.

Maternal Role Satisfaction

As mentioned above, the effects of a mother's work status on her child may be influenced by other factors in the mother, the child, and the context. For example, Marian Yarrow and her colleagues (Yarrow, Scott, deLeeuw, & Heinig, 1962) reported that if mothers were in their preferred roles they showed no differences in child-rearing; hence, it was role satisfaction, and not work status per se, that contributed to positive interactions with their children. In addition, Lois Hoffman (1963) reported differences on maternal, child, and teacher measures when comparing satisfied and dissatisfied employed mothers. The results of this study showed that satisfied mothers who were employed were perceived by their children as showing more positive affect and less severe discipline. In contrast, dissatisfied mothers perceived their children as more argumentative, and teachers reported the children as displaying assertive and sometimes hostile behavior in the classroom. More recently researchers have begun to realize the importance of maternal role satisfaction and the influence it has on child development, and have examined its influence in samples of employed and nonemployed mothers.

In addition to the early studies of Yarrow, Scott, deLeeuw, and Heinig (1962), and Hoffman (1963), the recent surge of interest in the literature on maternal role satisfaction has led to the idea that a mother's satisfaction with her role, whether she is employed or not, has positive effects on her children. In contrast, dissatisfaction is associated with negative effects on children. In elementary school children and adolescents, research findings show that congruence between the mother's attitude and her employment status leads to positive child outcomes (Baruch, 1972; Gold & Andres, 1978b; Lerner & Galambos, 1985; Pearlman, 1980; Williamson, 1970; Woods, 1972).

Research with infants and preschoolers has also led to the same conclusion with respect to congruence of mother's attitude and employment status. Ellen Hock (1980), for example, observed 12-month-old infants using the Strange Situation procedure. She found that infants who were less likely to maintain proximity with the mother during the stressful laboratory situation and who showed signs of conflict upon reunion with the mother were more likely to have mothers whose beliefs about the need of the infant for exclusive maternal care were not matched, or were incongruent with her work status. M. Francine Stuckey, Paul McGhee, and Nancy Bell (1982) found that incongruence between attitudes and maternal employment status is also related to parental behaviors. They reported that for a sample of preschoolers, both mothers and fathers were more likely to exhibit negative behaviors toward their children when the parents' attitudes were not matched with the mothers' work statuses.

Anita Farel (1980) also found that the most poorly adjusted children were those who had mothers who were nonemployed but wanted a job. There was no relationship between the mother's work status and school adjustment and competence; however, incongruence between the mother's attitude and her work status was related to lower competence in the child. In a similar vein, Margaret Owen, Lindsay Chase-Lansdale, and Michael Lamb (1984) reported that maternal work status was unrelated to the security of infant/mother or infant/father attachment. They found that the factor that did predict the security of infant attachment was the mothers' attitudes and values regarding parenthood and work.

A study with samples of both employed and nonemployed mothers and their preschool children (Lerner & Galambos, 1985) showed no differences in the children based on whether the mothers were employed or not, but relative to maternal role satisfaction, the study indicated that children of satisfied mothers were less difficult temperamentally than children of dissatisfied mothers. To discern the possible process involved in the link between maternal role satisfaction and child difficulty, the mother/child interaction was assessed. The mothers who were more satisfied were also more accepting of their children and displayed more warmth toward them than did the mothers who were dissatisfied. Hence, a possible process by which maternal role satisfaction may affect the child is through mother/child interaction.

Because these findings concur in suggesting that maternal role satisfaction and attitudes are linked more directly to child outcomes than is the mother's work status per se, many other researchers have also speculated about what underlying process may account for the positive child outcomes associated with the mother's role satisfaction and attitudes. Some have noted that role satisfaction and positive attitudes lead to positive parenting, which in turn enhances child development. Some studies have linked role satisfaction directly to child development outcomes (Farel, 1980; Hock, 1978, 1980; Hoffman, 1963; Williamson, 1970; Woods, 1972), whereas others link role satisfaction to parental functioning (Stuckey, McGhee, & Bell, 1982; Yarrow, Scott, deLeeuw, & Heinig, 1962). The manner in which role satisfaction may affect parenting has, however, been studied and discussed only recently in the literature. Lamb, Chase-Lansdale, and Owen (1979) proposed that role satisfaction leads to self-fulfillment and to the enhancement of self-esteem in the mother, which in turn leads her to be a more sensitive mother. Maternal sensitivity and responsiveness to an infant's cues have been found to be an important predictor of the quality of the mother/child relationship. As was mentioned earlier, role satisfaction has been linked to more warmth and acceptance of the child (Lerner & Galambos, 1985).

Differences in aspects of the mother/child relationship other than maternal responsiveness and warmth have also been linked to role satisfaction. Peter Warr and Glenys Parry (1982) found a general mood difference in employed mothers who are happy or unhappy with their job situations. They have found strong relationships among working-class women of the United Kingdom between employed mothers' overall attitudes toward their jobs and measures of positive and negative affect and life satisfaction. Mood differences may indeed become evident in parent/child interactions, as Stuckey, McGhee, and Bell (1982) found differences in parental affect expression according to attitude/employment congruence.

SOCIOEMOTIONAL DEVELOPMENT IN SCHOOL-AGE CHILDREN

As the child reaches school age, the issue of alternative care diminishes. However, how the school-age child spends time after school is of concern. Very few public schools have organized after-school programs, and therefore many children are spending their after-school hours unsupervised. These children have been popularly called "latchkey kids," but researchers prefer to call them children in self-care because of the negative connotations that have been previously associated with the term *latchkey*. It is estimated that 2.1 million children between the ages of 5 and 13 in the United States spend some part of the day in self-care because their mothers are employed. In terms of the influence of self-care on the school-age child, Nancy Galambos and Jennifer Maggs (1991) have summarized the research findings thus far. They conclude that the context of self-care is of utmost importance.

One question researchers have asked is whether self-care children show more advanced personal, social, or cognitive skills than children who are primarily in the care of adults. As a group, children in self-care do not show more of these skills. In addition, some forms of self-care may be conducive to the development of problem behavior. For example, when children spend their after-school hours away from home, they are more likely to associate with peers who get into trouble. However, self-care children who stay at home appear to be no different from adult-care children. Parental monitoring also makes a difference in the outcomes for self-care children. Laurence Steinberg (1986) found that parents are able to monitor their children from work and that when children have internalized values they are able to remain at home in a self-care situation without any negative consequences. He found that the children most susceptible to antisocial peer pressure were those who were either unsupervised and "hanging out" or unsupervised at a friend's home. Steinberg's findings point again to the need to look more closely at the context of self-care and how variations in context influence the child.

In addition to the issue of self-care, other research has evaluated the influence of maternal employment on the social development of school-age children. When a mother is employed, she provides a different role model for her children that affects the development of sex role stereotypes in these children. The children of employed mothers do have more egalitarian sex role concepts than the children of nonemployed mothers, and it seems that the self-concepts of daughters are positively affected by mothers' employment (Hoffman, 1974). In a study of children at three age levels—nursery school, age 10, and age 15—Dolores Gold and David Andres (1977) found that children of employed mothers have broader, less sex-typed concepts of males and females, and that this effect was strongest for the 10-year-olds.

Additionally, the mother/child interaction is affected because employed mothers are generally more satisfied (Hoffman, 1989). Children of mothers who are employed are generally more supportive of maternal employment, which also may contribute to preparing them for their own adult roles.

In general, for the school-age child who is adequately supervised, there seem to be social benefits of having a mother who is employed. Next is a discussion of how maternal employment influences the social development of adolescents.

SOCIOEMOTIONAL DEVELOPMENT IN ADOLESCENTS

One needs to carefully evaluate the developmental correlates of maternal employment during the period of adolescence. As mentioned previously, the needs of the adolescent are different from those of the younger child. Not only do adolescents need less attention from their mothers, but the employed mother may actually help her child's increasing needs for independence. In addition, the employed mother serves as a role model for both sons and daughters, for it is likely that daughters will be employed in their adult life and that sons will be married to employed women. In addition, during this developmental period, employed mothers may influence the development of their children's vocational and achievement aspirations.

There are other aspects of adolescent social development that appear to be affected by maternal employment. For example, adolescent daughters of employed mothers have less "fear of success" (Gilroy, Talierco, & Steinbacher, 1981) and a more positive concept of the female role (Hoffman, 1979). For boys, a less consistent pattern emerges. Some studies have suggested that boys of employed mothers are better adjusted than boys with nonemployed mothers (Gold & Andres, 1978a; Nelson, 1971; Trimberger & MacLean, 1982), but others report contradictory findings (McCord, McCord, & Thurber, 1963), or no differences at all (Burchinal, 1963; Dellas, Gaier, & Emihovich, 1979; Lerner & Galambos, 1988). These inconsistencies are partly a result of the direct effects approach. Simply comparing the adjustment of children from employed and nonemployed mother families ignores the other variables that can be affecting the adolescent.

For example, a major concern with adolescent children is how well their activities are supervised when their mothers are at work. The amount and type of supervision are critical factors in how the adolescent fares when the mother is employed. As mentioned earlier, Steinberg (1986) found that most children in self-care report that their parents know where they are after school. This long-distance supervision reduces the risk that self-care children have for greater susceptibility to negative peer pressure. Thus, the context of maternal employment provides more information about how the child is actually influenced.

In contrast to the research on young and school-age children, the direct effects approach to studying maternal employment influences has yielded evidence for global differences in the attributes of adolescents with employed and nonemployed mothers. For example, high school girls and college women with mothers who had histories of employment outside the home more often desired careers when compared to the daughters of nonemployed mothers (Almquist & Angrist, 1971; Altman & Grossman, 1977; Banducci, 1967; Stein, 1973). Moreover, studies of adult women with doctorates found that those most likely to be employed after receiving their degrees were daughters of mothers who were employed outside the home (Astin, 1969). Other research has shown that adolescent girls and college women who were preparing for male-dominated occupations were more likely to be the daughters of employed mothers than those who preferred typically feminine occupations (Almquist, 1974; Douvan, 1963; Tangri, 1972). Grace Baruch (1972), however, found no differences related to maternal employment with respect to occupational aspirations in college women.

There is also evidence supporting stronger aspirations for a higher level of education among high school boys and girls whose mothers were employed (Banducci, 1967; Roy, 1963). Researchers have reported that college females with employed mothers had higher educational aspirations than those whose mothers were not employed (Stein, 1973). In another study, maternal employment was not associated with any differences in the educational or vocational aspirations of adolescent boys and girls (Gold & Andres, 1978a).

Generally, the mother's employment is associated with fewer sex role stereotypes—beliefs that particular behaviors or attributes are characteristic of one sex group as opposed to another (Lerner & Hultsch, 1983)—held by daughters and sons. This has been found to be true in early adolescents (Bacon & Lerner, 1975), adolescents (Chandler, Sawicki, & Struffler, 1981; Gold & Andres, 1978a), and college students (Vogel, Broverman, Broverman, Clarkson, & Rosenkrantz, 1970).

Moreover, adolescent and college-age children of employed mothers tend to be more achievement-oriented than do the children of homemaker mothers (Powell, 1963; Stein, 1973), suggesting a relationship between maternal employment and masculine personality dimensions. The sex role attitudes of preadolescent, adolescent, and college-age sons and daughters with employed mothers on the whole tend to be more egalitarian than these attitudes in children with homemaker mothers (Dellas, Gaier, & Emihovich, 1979; King, McIntyre, & Axelson, 1968; Meier, 1972; VanFossen, 1977). This means that children with employed mothers approve more of equality between men and women with respect to roles, responsibilities, and behaviors.

In addition, there is evidence that maternal employment may be related to the degree to which individuals describe themselves as having masculine and feminine personality characteristics (i.e., sex role identity). Female undergraduates are more likely to report having both feminine and masculine traits (i.e., possessing androgyny) if their mothers are employed (Hansson, Chernovetz, & Jones, 1977). Elizabeth Douvan (1963) found that adolescent girls described themselves as less feminine when their mothers were employed. These research findings point to overall group differences in adolescents and young adults with employed and nonemployed mothers. Those individuals with employed mothers may be said to have less sex-typed attributes than those with nonemployed mothers.

There have been some attempts to go beyond the direct effects approach in evaluating the influence of maternal employment on adolescent development. Some studies have investigated the variable of maternal role satisfaction and aspects of adolescent development. In some of these the results are not clearly interpretable or the methodology used is deficient in some respect. Delores Gold and David Andres (1978a), for instance, reported that employed mothers of adolescents in their sample were more satisfied with their roles than were nonemployed mothers. These investigators, however, did not report whether maternal role satisfaction was related to any aspects of the adolescent's development that were studied.

A more precise study of a mother's affect or satisfaction and adolescent outcome was done by Joebgen and Richards (1990). They found that when the mother's educational level matches her employment status, higher self-esteem results for the mothers. When the mother's affect is positive, adolescent children report more positive affect. Thus, there is some support for the link between the mother's role satisfaction and adolescent adjustment, but it is a weaker link than the one found with younger children. Nancy Galambos, Anne Petersen, and Kathleen Lenerz (1988) have explained this weaker link by noting that maternal role satisfaction may more strongly influence the nature of the mother/child relationship when the child is young, but the diminished contact between the mother and child in adolescence also may diminish the maternal role satisfaction/child adjustment link.

Other factors in the family environment have been investigated in the examination of the relationship between maternal employment and adolescent development. Maryse Richards and Elena Duckett (1991) noted that the family environment is probably still the most critical variable that mediates the impact of maternal employment on adolescent development. The variables of importance change slightly from the ones that were important in infancy and early childhood. For example, maternal employment means some decrease in maternal availability, but this will affect the infant and adolescent differently.

Although the total amount of time spent with family decreases during adolescence, Reed Larson and Maryse Richards (1991) found that maternal employment does not necessarily reduce the amount of time spent with parents. Raymond Montemayor (1984), on the other hand, found that teens spend less time with their mothers when their mothers are employed. There has not been enough research to conclude whether maternal employment is associated with less contact between mothers and their teenage children.

In studies that have looked at maternal availability and do find decreases when the mother is employed, boys appear to be more vulnerable. Some studies that have found negative effects for boys have attributed it to a lack of parental supervision and structure. Parents may tend to assume that boys need less supervision than girls, and maternal employment may increase the lack of supervision. Adolescent boys, however, have been found to need more supervision and monitoring than girls (Bronfenbrenner & Crouter, 1982) and therefore may be more vulnerable to adverse influences of maternal employment.

Family interaction and children's perceptions of their parents may also be influenced by maternal employment. Some research has found that there are no differences between employed- and nonemployed-mother families in children's perceptions of their parents (Rosenthal & Hansen, 1981). In addition, Lois Hoffman (1979) proposed that maternal employment during the child's adolescence leads to better mother/child relations, especially for girls, because it encourages their autonomy. Also, because of an increased role in household responsibilities when their mothers are employed, adolescent children may feel more involved with their families. However, there has also been evidence for an increase in family conflict when older adolescents feel burdened by the additional responsibility (Trimberger & MacLean, 1982).

The above effects seem to be moderated, in some studies, by the number of hours that the mother works. For example, some researchers found that the closest mother-child relations were reported by daughters whose mothers were employed part-time (Douvan & Adelson, 1966). They note that part-time employment may be optimal in that the child had both maternal availability and the competent role model. In single-mother families, opposing findings emerge. In these families, more positive adjustment in adolescent children is associated with mother's full-time employment. Elena Duckett and Maryse Richards (1989) found also that in their sample of single mothers, mothers' full-time employment is associated with higher affect reported by children, as well as more positive perceptions and feelings about their fathers. Thus, the complexity of the maternal employment/child development link continues into adolescence; however, new variables take on importance during this period.

SUMMARY

In terms of the socioemotional development of infants, preschoolers, school-age children, and adolescents, there does not seem to be any direct, consistent influences of maternal employment. Research on infant samples is typically done in day-care centers. This research shows mixed results, but no global, adverse effects of day care. Socially, children in day-care settings seem to interact more with their peers in both positive and negative ways. The impact of day care on the mother/child relationship is a controversial issue. Most studies have used the Strange Situation paradigm to assess this relationship, and many have found problems with this paradigm. The quality of infant/mother attachment and infant socioemotional development is dependent on many factors in the child's day-care setting and family. Researchers need to evaluate the quality of the day-care experience and the family environment of the infant when studying how maternal employment may be linked to infant development. These factors are also important as the child ages.

For preschoolers, studies find no general differences in employed and nonemployed groups. It seems that as the child ages, other variables associated with maternal education and maternal role satisfaction play an important role in child development. As children reach school age, researchers are concerned with how they are supervised after school when their mothers are employed. It appears that as long as children are monitored and have positive family environments, there are no adverse effects of self-care. Maternal employment does seem to influence the sex role stereotypes of school-age children and adolescents. Children of employed mothers have more egalitarian sex role concepts than the children of nonemployed mothers, and the daughter's self-concept is positively affected by her mother's employment. In addition, the increased independence of the older child seems to go well with maternal employment. Employed mothers are more willing to encourage independence in their children, and this has beneficial effects for both the mother and the child. Maternal employment is also associated with stronger aspirations for both sons and daughters. Researchers are continuing to sort out the complex nature of the link between maternal employment and child development.

REVIEW QUESTIONS

1. What are some of the problems with doing research on day-care samples to evaluate the influence of maternal employment on infants and young children?
2. What are the limitations of the Strange Situation assessment in research on day care?
3. How has maternal role satisfaction been implicated in the relationship between maternal employment and child development?
4. How do the variables of interest in maternal employment research change across the child's life?

SUGGESTED PROJECTS

1. Obtain permission to observe in one or two day-care centers or preschools in your community. Using the list in Table 4.1, evaluate the quality of these centers.
2. Interview some high school boys and girls about their attitudes regarding maternal employment. Determine whether they hold traditional or nontraditional sex role attitudes and see if their attitudes are related to whether their own mothers are employed.

CHAPTER

5

Maternal Employment and Children's Educational and Vocational Choices

Do CHILDREN GROW UP and follow in their parents' footsteps? Does the old saying, "like father, like son" ring true for most of today's youth? I am sure that you remember "playing house" as a youngster, imitating your parents, whether they were dentists, office managers, waitresses, or homemakers. Whether or not these early imitating behaviors of children actually result in conscious educational and vocational choices is a question that social scientists studying employment have tried to answer.

As previously discussed, new issues arise when exploring the relationship between maternal employment and the development of older children and adolescents. Although concern for the child's emotional, social, and intellectual development is still important, factors such as the child's educational and vocational choices also assume importance. Of course, these choices are also influenced by variables other than whether the mother is employed. Maternal and paternal attitudes, occupational status, and the socioeconomic status of the family are all factors to consider.

The mechanisms by which a mother's employment status may influence her children are complex. Some of these complexities have been noted in the previous chapters. For example, the mother's role satisfaction seems to play an important part in the young child's development when the mother is employed, and this continues into the child's adolescence. In general, when a mother has a satisfactory employment situation, she is more likely to transmit a positive attitude about employment to her child. From a role-modeling perspective, this should affect the child's attitudes about employment in a positive way. In addition, maternal role satisfaction should also translate into more positive mother/child interactions, which should enhance the child's development in general.

A mother's educational level may also influence a child's educational and occupational choices, as children of highly educated mothers may set higher goals for themselves. Highly educated mothers are more likely to be employed, but the influence of maternal education on children needs to be evaluated in both employed and nonemployed mother samples.

This chapter is concerned mainly with examining the role that maternal employment plays in the educational and vocational attainment of children. A section on the influences of paternal employment is included in addition because in recent years research has been directed also at the major role that fathers play in child development.

INFLUENCING CHILDREN'S ATTITUDES

How a mother's employment status may influence her child's attitudes regarding educational and career attainment depends on many factors. First, the age at which the child first experiences his or her mother's employment may play a role in the attitudes that develop. It may be that the earlier a child experiences maternal employment, the more likely it is for the child to believe that employment is a usual and viable part of a woman's life. Of course, the child's attitudes are also thought to be shaped by the socioeconomic status and race of the family, although there is not compelling evidence that this is the case (Banducci, 1967; Gold & Andres, 1978a). Lois Hoffman (1974) has pointed out that in some families the additional income generated by the mother's employment may allow the child to advance educationally. In this way, maternal income may have a more direct role in the educational progress of the child.

The influence of maternal income on the child's educational progress is confounded by the fact that a mother's higher earnings are related to her own education, work involvement, and

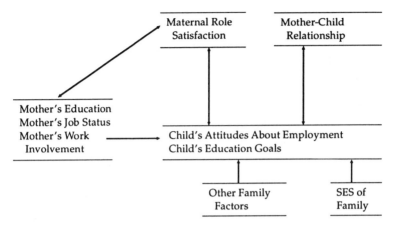

Figure 5.1. Maternal and Family Factors and Their Potential Influence on Children's Employment Attitudes and Educational Goals

higher status employment. Thus, we see once again that the way in which maternal employment influences any aspect of child development is complex. Figure 5.1 presents a chart of some of the factors that could be involved in this influence.

MATERNAL EMPLOYMENT AND CHILDREN'S SEX ROLE ATTITUDES

Although chapter 4 discussed the research that relates maternal employment to sex role development in adolescents, reviewing it here is useful because a child's sex role attitudes will influence his or her educational and vocational aspirations and choices. Studies that have considered the influence of maternal employment on the sex role attitudes of younger children will also be examined in this chapter.

Overall, studies have frequently found that children of employed mothers have less restricted views of sex roles than do children of nonemployed mothers. Martha Zaslow (1987) and Lois Hoffman (1989) have found that this seems to be the case for children from kindergarten age to adulthood. Grace Baruch (1972) and Elizabeth Douvan (1963) have found that in daughters especially, maternal employment has been associated with a more positive and broader definition of the female role. These daughters report a greater admiration of their mothers and show more independence than daughters of nonemployed mothers.

The picture regarding sex role development and perceptions is not as strong for boys. Whereas the studies reported above have found more liberal sex role perceptions in the sons of employed mothers, Dolores Gold and Davis Andres (1978a) have found no differences. This finding may be explained through role model theory—that daughters will be affected more in their attitudes because their primary role models and sources of identification are their mothers.

In research on college women conducted by Elizabeth Almquist and Shirley Angrist (1971), daughters were more likely to be career-oriented if their mothers were employed. Similar studies of college women have shown that those who aspired to less traditional careers were also more likely to have employed mothers (Tangri, 1972). With younger children, similar results have emerged (Banducci, 1967; Smith, 1969). Grace Baruch (1972), however, found that daughters of employed mothers had aspirations for combining employment and motherhood, but only when they perceived that the combination of these roles for their mothers did not result in high levels of stress. Hence maternal stress, role strain, and role satisfaction can influence the role that maternal employment has on daughters' career aspirations.

Complicating the picture are the studies that fail to find this effect with older adolescents. Some researchers have found that maternal employment was related to nontraditional sex role attitudes in children of elementary school age but not for early adolescents (Chandler, Sawicki, & Struffler, 1981; Marantz & Mansfield, 1977). Raymond Montemayor and Mark Clayton (1983) have speculated that the peer group may be more of an influence in shaping the sex role concepts of the adolescent than is maternal employment status. Because of these contrasting results, more research is obviously needed to examine the nature and course of the influence of maternal employment on children's sex role attitudes.

MATERNAL EMPLOYMENT AND
CHILDREN'S VOCATIONAL BEHAVIORS

Once the child's attitudes have been influenced by the mother's own employment status, attitudes, and behaviors, there is the question of how these attitudes are translated into the actual behaviors of the child; that is, do daughters of employed mothers actually attain a higher level of education or choose careers that are less traditional? Do they postpone marriage and childbearing in order to solidify their status in the labor market? Does a mother's employment affect the child's educational goals and alter the child's occupational knowledge base in a way that makes it possible for the child to eventually be a viable part of the labor force?

Some of these questions were addressed by Ronald D'Amico, R. Jean Haurin, and Frank Mott (1983). They used the National Longitudinal Surveys of Labor Market Experience, which followed young women and men through their late adolescent years, and examined a number of educational, career, and family outcomes in relation the mother's employment experiences (Center for Human Resource Research, 1982). Thus, this data set is rich in that it allows some of the above questions to be addressed with longitudinal data.

D'Amico, Haurin, and Mott (1983) used outcomes collected when the respondents were 24 to 27 years old. They found that in terms of maternal education, when mothers attained higher levels of education, the more likely it was for daughters to have higher educational aspirations, to take nontraditional courses in high school, to have greater occupational knowledge, and to work while in high school. This finding provides evidence for the intergenerational transmission of both attitudes and behaviors regarding nontraditional roles for daughters. Both mothers' and fathers' nontraditional attitudes regarding women's roles and their support of such roles are seen in daughters' own attitudes and behaviors. This finding did not hold for sons; only fathers' occupational status scores bore any relation to nontraditionalism for sons.

Educational Attainment

In terms of actual educational attainment, D'Amico, Haurin, and Mott (1983) found a consistent pattern for the effect of the mother's highest grade completed. Highly educated mothers were found to have children who, in general, completed more schooling; that is, they had sons who were more likely to complete high school and attend college and daughters who were more likely to attend and complete college. Interestingly, there was no indication in this sample that the prestige of the mother's occupation influenced the status of the daughter's job. However, there was a significant influence of the mothers' work commitment on daughters' intentions to work; that is, mothers who said that they would work even if they did not have to financially had daughters who planned to work at age 35.

This finding is consistent with the idea that it matters less that a mother is employed or in what type of profession she is employed, and more that if she is satisfied with her role, she is likely to pass on her own work commitment attitudes to her daughter. In terms of influencing daughters' nontraditionalism, the more nontraditional a mother's sex role attitude is, the more nontraditional the daughter's is, the fewer the number of children she expects to have, the fewer the number of children she has given birth to at age 24, and the more likely she is to express the intention to be employed at age 35. For sons in this data set a surprising finding emerges—fathers' and mothers' nontraditionalism are associated with more traditional attitudes. Perhaps this finding has to do with the fact that these sons experienced their parents' nontraditionalism during a historical period when the majority of mothers were not in the labor force (during the 1960s and 1970s). Sons may have felt as if they were in the minority if their mothers were employed, and thus may have held more traditional attitudes. This is speculative, however, because this finding does not hold in all studies that examine sons' attitudes.

In thinking about the findings of D'Amico, Haurin, and Mott (1983), keep in mind that the data set examined the influences of maternal employment on children between the late 1950s to about 1970. Although having the opportunity to examine these influences in such a complete longitudinal data set is rare, the social attitudes of those decades and the reasons that women were employed were quite different from what they are today.

Today maternal employment is the norm, and although there are still those who disagree with it, most people accept its prevalence. The economic realities of the world are more likely to influence parents' expectations for both sons and daughters as well as children's expectations for themselves.

The Importance of the Context

It is useful to reiterate here the importance of considering the context when studying the influences of maternal employment on any aspect of child development. The previous chapters have shown that variations in the home, the family, and the social setting as well as the child all will moderate the influence that maternal employment has on child development. Some of the variables that have been shown to moderate the influence of maternal employment on children's educational attainment and aspirations, sex role stereotypes, and career choices for daughters are race, social class, parental support, father's occupational success, and family size. The next section discusses the influences of paternal employment on children.

PATERNAL EMPLOYMENT
AND CHILD DEVELOPMENT

Psychologist Julian Barling (1991) stated that there is "a dearth of empirical research on the effects of fathers' employment on father-child interactions and their children's behavior" (p. 181). This lack of research is in contrast to the surge of empirical activity that has been devoted to an examination of the impact of maternal employment on children's development. There are good reasons for this lack of research.

First, the breadwinning role traditionally ascribed to fathers carries with it the expectation that fathers will be absent from the home and from their children in order to hold a full-time job to provide for the welfare of the family. Because the absence of the father is expected and the livelihood of the family depends on his employment, there has not been much concern over whether a father's employment-related absence is in any way detrimental to the child. In fact, more concern has centered around paternal unemployment.

Second, although some research has examined the intergenerational transmission of occupational choices between fathers and sons, this research has not focused on the influence of the father's occupation and experiences on other aspects of child development. This stems partly from the ideology that it is the mother who is the primary caregiver and therefore the major influence on the development of the child. In addition to the ideology that assumes no influence of paternal employment on children, research has been further hampered by the fact that it is impossible to compare groups of children whose fathers are voluntarily nonemployed to groups of children whose fathers are employed.

Currently, there is an increasing interest in the role that fathers' employment plays in child behaviors, and in father/child interaction. Julian Barling (1991) has noted several reasons for this increased interest. With the work of psychologists such as Michael Lamb (1981, 1982), the role of the father in child development has been under more systematic empirical scrutiny in the past decades and research has supported the importance of the father's role. In addition, maternal employment has become the norm, and even in the most traditional families, fathers have had to become more involved in child care and parenting. Finally, maternal employment research has made us aware of the notion that employment per se may not be the most critical variable influencing child development. The mother's subjective experiences, role satisfaction, and role strain have become the important variables, thus making it possible to also examine these variables in fathers.

Fathers' Job-Related Absences

Because fathers are expected to be absent from their children in order to work, there is little research that has examined the influence of ordinary job-related father absence on children. The normative absence of fathers is not thought to exert any detrimental effects on children; in fact, C. Piotrkowski and L. Gornick (1987) have proposed that because ordinary job-related absences are predictable and temporary, children adapt to them easily. However, extraordinary absences such as prolonged naval tours of duty (Marsella, Dubanoski, & Mohs, 1974), may differentially influence the child.

Studies have found effects of prolonged, extraordinary job-related absences on mother/child interaction and child behavior. For example, some researchers (Marsella, Dubanoski, & Mohs, 1974) have postulated that father absence affects children indirectly through its effect on the mother. Mothers whose husbands are away for long periods of time may change their attitudes and childrearing practices. In addition, they may show more signs of stress that may influence their interactions with their children. This effect was indeed found by Marsella, Dubanoski, and Mohs (1974). Mothers were more dominant with their children when their husbands were present than when they were away, perhaps because fathers who are away for long periods overcompensate when they are home, and mothers feel the need to retain some control. This inconsistency in parenting from mothers may not be beneficial to mother/child interactions because it confuses the child in reading the mother's style and in anticipating her responses.

Mothers have also been found to be more depressed when their husbands were away due to their employment (Beckman, Marsella, & Finney, 1979). This alteration in maternal mood may also affect the interactions mothers have with their children and thus influence child behavior and development. One has to be careful in generalizing these findings to nonmilitary samples, but these studies do provide an idea that prolonged father absence due to employment may have some effect on both the mother and the child.

In a sample of nonmilitary families in rural Australia, John Cotterell (1986) examined whether fathers' prolonged job absences (due to shift work or traveling) influenced mothers' childrearing attitudes. He found that in the sample of mothers whose husbands were frequently away, the mothers played with their children less and provided less cognitive stimulation than the comparison group of mothers whose husbands were not absent frequently. This finding may be a result of the increased amount of household tasks that the mother is responsible for during her husband's absence. In any event, it seems clear that fathers' prolonged job-related absences in some way influences mothers' attitudes, childrearing practices, and interactions with their children.

Paternal Employment and Child Behaviors

In terms of the behaviors of the child, studies have looked at whether the father's prolonged job-related absences influence the child's intellectual development or social behavior. Elizabeth Hillenbrand (1976) found that the longer the father was away, the higher were sons' quantitative abilities, particularly for firstborn sons. This study was the only one of its type to find this relationship; therefore the interpretation must be cautious. Barling (1991) has speculated that it may indicate the tendency for firstborn sons to show intellectual superiority, especially after periods of hardship (father absence), because of the added responsibility that they take on during that absence.

David Lynn and William Sawrey (1959) investigated whether job-related father absence influenced children's social behaviors in a sample of Norwegian sailors. When contrasted with a group of children whose fathers were continuously present, the researchers found that the children of the sailors were less mature, more poorly adjusted, and had less secure identification with their fathers. Again, one must be careful in interpreting these results because other variables such as socioeconomic status, type of paternal job, or personality characteristics of the fathers may be playing roles in the children's behaviors.

Barling (1991) cautions again about the meaning of these studies, which seem to indicate some negative effects of prolonged job-related father absence on children and wives. He makes the point that has been made continuously in this book; that is, the need to look beyond the employment status of the father and investigate the father's subjective experiences such as job satisfaction. Also, one must take into consideration the meaning that the father's absences have for the child, the mother, and the father himself. Barling's own research has documented that consistent with similar research on maternal employment, the father's subjective experiences and the meaning of employment are more important determinants of marital functioning (Barling, 1990) and children's problem behavior (Barling, 1986) than employment per se. Specifically, Barling (1986) found that fathers' job dissatisfaction was associated with children's conduct problems and hyperactivity.

A Process Model of Employment Effects

Barling's research is in line with the model advanced to account for the link between maternal role dissatisfaction and child problems (Lerner & Galambos, 1985). He asserts (as do Lerner & Galambos, 1985), that job dissatisfaction influences the way in which fathers interact with their children. These interactions more directly affect the child than any aspect of the employment. In order to test this assertion, Frances Grossman, William Pollack, and Ellen Golding (1988) used role satisfaction and job involvement to predict aspects of the father/child relationship in a sample of 5-year-old children and their fathers. They found that the higher the father's job satisfaction, the less time spent with the children. However, they only assessed quantity of time, not quality. Donald McKinley's work (1964) has looked at the quality of the father/child interaction and has found that the father's job dissatisfaction predicts hostility toward the child and more severe disciplinary techniques (McKinley, 1964; Kemper & Reichler, 1976). Similarly, others have found (Grossman, Pollack, & Golding, 1988) that fathers' job satisfaction was positively related to their support of their children's autonomy and affiliation.

Piotrkowski and Stark (1987) and Barling (1986) have advanced a rationale as to why the father's role satisfaction or dissatisfaction affects child behavior through the quality of the father/child relationship. Children who are in a close relationship with their fathers are given the opportunity to know and understand the dissatisfaction and how it is affecting their father. They therefore are in a better position to be affected by it. Barling (1986) has provided data to support this rationale. He found that the father's job dissatisfaction was more likely to be associated with problems in the child if there was a close father/child relationship. Of course, for both maternal and paternal employment, more research is needed to identify the specific job experiences that influence children's behavior through job dissatisfaction and the parent/child relationship.

FATHERS' INFLUENCE ON SONS' OCCUPATIONAL CHOICES

How a mother's employment status and occupation may influence her children's choices was discussed earlier in this chapter. Along these lines, many studies have evaluated whether children choose the same or similar occupations of their fathers. In a series of early studies (Nelson, 1939; Jensen & Kirschner, 1955; Aberle & Naegele, 1952; Werts, 1968) the link between fathers' and sons' occupations was demonstrated. However, these studies did not provide any insight as to why this link is so strong.

There have been subsequent attempts to determine how fathers actually influence their sons' occupational choices. Breakwell, Fife-Schaw, and Devereux (1988) tested whether fathers may engage in deliberate, conscious behaviors to influence their children's choices. They asked teenagers whether their fathers had deliberately tried to influence their occupational choices and whether their fathers were successful. Although the teenagers reported that their fathers had tried to influence them, they did so unsuccessfully. Barling (1991) has noted that perhaps the teenagers are inclined to deny that their parents influence their behavior in any way and suggests caution in the interpretation of these results.

Others studies point to an indirect influence of fathers on sons' choices of occupations. Using Melvin Kohn's (1977) assumption that a father's occupational values will influence his son's attitudes and behavior, Jeylan Mortimer (1974) and her colleagues (Mortimer, Lorence, & Kumka, 1986) demonstrated that sons' occupational preferences matched their fathers' occupations, and for those that did not match exactly, the sons' occupations were similar in value structures to those of their fathers' occupations. This research also found that when the father/child relationship was close, the occupational linkages between father and son were stronger. Hence, the quality of the parent/child relationship is an influential part of the process by which parental work affects the child.

SUMMARY

The mechanisms by which maternal employment influences children's educational and vocational choices are complex. Mothers do transmit their own attitudes about work to their children, especially to their daughters. Both daughters and sons of employed women tend to have less restricted views of sex roles than children of nonemployed women. Whether these views are translated into actual behaviors has become a matter of empirical concern; that is, are daughters more likely to be career-oriented and do they actually make educational choices consistent with this orientation if their mothers are employed?

Research does tend to support the link between maternal employment and daughters' attitudes, aspirations, and behaviors. Many studies have found that women aspire to less traditional careers, have higher educational goals, and are more likely to plan to combine employment and motherhood if their mothers are employed. However, other variables come into play, as they do when evaluating the influence of maternal employment on other child outcomes. For example, daughters report the desire to combine work and motherhood when they perceive that this combination did not result in high levels of stress for their mothers. Maternal role satisfaction and work commitment play a similar mediating role. The subjective experiences of employment play a role in how a mother's employment attitudes and behaviors affect her child. More satisfied mothers not only transmit a more positive, less stressed role model to their children, but they are more likely to be able to have more positive interactions with their children in general, thus enhancing the child's development.

A similar relationship is found in studies examining the influence of paternal employment on children. Again, the father's subjective work experiences and the father/child relationship play a more important role in the child's development than the actual employment. Extraordinary absences of the father due to employment have been found to have an influence on the mother, her interactions with her child, and the child's behaviors. However, research has begun to consider the influence of paternal work satisfaction and the father/child relationship when examining the paternal employment/child development link.

REVIEW QUESTIONS

1. In general, what are the links between maternal employment and daughters' sex role development?
2. Name some of the complex ways in which maternal employment is related to children's vocational and educational choices.
3. Are there any indications from research that maternal employment and paternal employment may influence children in similar ways?
4. What are some of the differences in the influences of maternal employment for daughters and sons?

SUGGESTED PROJECTS

1. Get a group of college students together and discuss whether they plan to choose careers similar to their parents'. Determine if females tend to choose careers similar to their mothers' and if males choose careers similar to their fathers'.
2. Interview your mother or father about various aspects of their jobs. Ask them to point out both positive and negative characteristics.

6

Maternal Employment and Social Policy: What Do We Have? What Is Missing?

YOU SHOULD BE CONVINCED by now that maternal employment is a feature of family life that is here to stay. As you embark on your careers and family life, you will be faced with the questions that young people have asked for years about combining work and family. These questions may include: Should I stay home with my baby? Should I work part-time until he or she is in school? Should I use at-home or center child care? Should I put off my career until I have raised my children? Should I sacrifice career goals to raise my children? Can we make ends meet with only one of us working?

The difference for young people today is that it is becoming less of a choice for women to be employed or not. The economic situation is such that fewer women will be able to make the choice to stay at home with their children without incurring financial burdens. The increases in educational and career opportunities for women will add to the social acceptance of maternal employment. In addition, because researchers have been better able to evaluate the effects of both maternal employment and day care on children, there will be greater awareness of the factors that do influence children when their mothers are employed and changes can be made in family life that will serve to benefit each family member.

Benefits for family members include the supports given to employed mothers by employers, communities, and government. Mothers who are employed for whatever reasons are concerned about the availability of competitive jobs with health care benefits and maternal leave policies. They are also concerned with the availability of high-quality child care in their community, and with the potential expense.

This chapter will elaborate on these concerns and discuss how they have been translated into community, employer, and governmental supports. It will present what exists for employed mothers, and what is lacking. Several areas will be explored: Child care, parental leave, flexible work arrangements, and future needs.

CHILD CARE

For employed-mother families with young children, a major concern is with the availability, affordability, and quality of child care. Finding high-quality child care that is affordable is a difficult task. Because research has documented that out-of-home care needs to be of high-quality (educationally and emotionally stimulating) in order for children to benefit, more high-quality care needs to be made affordable and available to families of all socioeconomic groups.

Infant Care

Because infant care is both the most expensive and the least available, additional governmental attention needs to be focused on this concern. For instance, efforts need to be directed at making infant care more affordable for lower income groups. As it stands now, only a small percentage of families can afford the $400-600 per month tuition for high-quality center-based infant care. Child-care centers cannot afford to introduce sliding fee scales based on income level because the cost of maintaining high-quality care is so high. Public policy needs to step in, not only as a means of support for lower income families, but because high-quality care is essential for healthy child developmental outcomes. The employed-mother family is not going to disappear; it has to be recognized as a part of this culture and dealt with in the most beneficial way for all parties concerned.

Government Attempts at Child-Care Policies

A traditional way that government policymakers have dealt with child care in the past has been to ignore it. Minor attempts to subsidize care for lower income families have been inconsistent and short-lived. In addition to the high cost of care, staff turnover rate for child-care workers is 42% annually, almost double the rate for other occupations (O'Connell & Bachu, 1988). The low pay, lack of benefits, low status, and long hours all contribute to this high turnover. Because this inconsistency in staff compromises the quality of care, it is essential that policymakers analyze the child-care profession and make adjustments to insure a more stable, high-status, higher paying profession.

Additional efforts need to be directed toward licensing. It is the responsibility of public agencies to assess whether child-care programs meet minimum standards of quality and safety. There is a need to encourage enrollment in quality programs, to enhance the training of child-care staff, and to assist all providers in satisfying licensing criteria. Even if all of these efforts were to be realized, affordability would still be an issue for the average family. High-quality child care and supervision should be continually on the minds of social policymakers so that child care becomes financially supported because it is viewed as every child's right.

Child Care for Older Children

The issue of child care does not end when we talk about older children. Before- and after-school care are concerns for employed parents of school-age children. Research on both early- and mid-adolescent children has found that the type of after-school supervision a child experiences is more critical than whether or not the mother is employed (Galambos & Maggs, 1991).

The type of care that will benefit children of this age depends somewhat on the characteristics of the child. Some older, more mature, and responsible children are adequately supervised by a phone call from a parent, just to "check in," allowing them to get on with the afternoon routine. Other children who are not as responsible, or younger children, may need the more structured and direct supervision of an after-school program. These programs are not widely available, and where they are available the expense is prohibitive to most families below the middle-income range. Throughout the latter part of the 1980s, Congress debated the need for comprehensive child-care legislation and appropriations. Two related child-care bills have been enacted by Congress to help lower income families deal with the financial burden of child care. One of these bills, the Child Care and Development Block Grant (U.S. Department of Health and Human Services, 1991), provides over $730 million nationally for early childhood development, child care, and before- and after-school services. The grant allows parents to select the providers of the care and gives these lower income families and their children a chance to fulfill their economic potential and the developmental potential of their children.

More needs to be done, however, because the most recent U.S. Bureau of the Census (1987) survey found that about 2.1 million children between the ages of 5 and 13 were regularly left unsupervised by an adult after school in 1984. Availability of programs needs to increase. For many middle-income families who could afford the services, there are no services to be found. Schools are the most obvious place for before- and after-school care, yet many school districts have not taken notice of the services they could provide (for profit) to many families.

Employer Efforts at Child-Care Policies

The major problem that faces those in the public arena who want to make changes in child-care policy is time. Debates can go on for years, and solutions can take even longer. There is still no broad-based policy on child care, and a federal parental leave policy was not established until 1993. Employers can, however, begin to contribute significantly to the quality of life of working families. Individual employers are beginning to enhance their ability to recruit workers and strengthen their competitive edge by offering a variety of child-care options and benefits (Lerner & Abrams, in press).

Employer Child-Care Options

Some employer child-care options include (a) before- and after-school programs and summer camps; (b) cafeteria benefit plans that allow employees to select taxable and nontaxable coverages from a "menu"; (c) on- or near-site child-care centers; (d) vouchers and reimbursement programs; (e) dependent care plans that allow employees to pay for child care with pretax dollars and grant tax deductions to participating employers; (f) emergency and sick child care; (g) family day-care networks that provide substitute caregivers and group discounts; (h) information, education, and referrals to licensed programs; and (i) support for local centers and agencies.

When employers have assisted their employees with child care, they report that they have reduced turnover and absenteeism, are in a better position to recruit, and enjoy good public relations and improved morale (Place, 1987). With these advantages it is surprising that only a small percentage of employers have such programs in place.

PARENTAL LEAVE

Over 93% of women in the work force who are in their prime childbearing years will become pregnant at some point in their working lives (Schroeder, 1988). Because more than 80% of women in the work force are in their prime childbearing years, the number of women who will need maternity benefits is enormous. Government leaders have finally realized the importance of this issue, and there is now a federal policy for family and medical leave. Leave is still unpaid, which means that not all families can take advantage of the policy.

The United States is years behind other countries of the western world with respect to paid maternity or parental leave. For example, as of 1987, the countries of Norway, Austria, Germany, Portugal, and the Netherlands had policies of at least 3 months of paid leave at 100% salary. Sweden has a policy of 9 months' leave at 90% salary and an additional 3 months at a flat rate. Denmark

and France have policies of at least 16 weeks at 90% salary, and
Finland has a policy of 11 months at 80% salary. This list goes on
for many more countries, and for a majority of those mentioned,
the benefit is also available to fathers.

For employers that have instituted some sort of leave policy,
parental leave is usually unpaid (as it is in the new federal policy)
and guarantees the job security of workers needing time off to
care for a newborn, newly adopted, or seriously ill child. Disability leave is paid or unpaid and covers the time during which a
woman is physically disabled after childbirth. Maternity leave is
usually unpaid leave granted to mothers for an extended period
at the end of disability leave so that they can care for their infants
(Lerner & Abrams, in press).

In 1978, federal attention to the issue of pregnancy was dealt
with by the passage of the Pregnancy Discrimination Act, an
amendment to the Civil Rights Act. This act prohibits sex discrimination by employers on the basis of pregnancy and requires
that pregnancy be treated like any other disability. It mandates
companies to include pregnancy and maternity in their disability
plan, *if* the company has a plan.

Many changes since 1978 have rendered the Pregnancy Discrimination Act an inadequate attempt at resolving the nation's
family leave needs. Since the time of the act, over half of the
women with children have entered or returned to the work force,
part-time employment without benefits has become a national
pattern for employed women who are also raising a family, and
the cost of health benefits has aroused national concern. Despite
the obvious need for a formal system of family support policies,
many employers have none.

A Congressional debate began in the late 1980s with the hope
that some progress could be made to resolve the discrepancies
between the needs of families and the supports of employers.
Until January 1993, the United States was the only industrialized
country without a national parental leave policy. Unfortunately,
it remains the view of many in government that mothers should
remain at home to care exclusively for their children during the
child's early years. Even though the research evidence to support
the idea that infants need exclusive mothering is lacking, many

still adhere to the notion that the separation of the mother and infant will adversely affect parenting and the child's development in the long run (Lerner & Abrams, in press).

The employed-mother situation in the United States will not change, however, and employed mothers must arrange for the management of their households and family lives after the arrival of a new family member. Employers need to pay attention to the fact that a lack of support on their part for employed mothers will undoubtedly lead to stress, absenteeism, poor performance, and the like. The advantages of placing the needs of employed mothers in a prominent position in the current debate cannot be underestimated.

SOCIAL POLICY AND
MATERNAL ROLE SATISFACTION

The research reviewed in this chapter points clearly to the fact that maternal behavior toward children is enhanced when the mother is in her preferred role. That role can be homemaking or employment outside the home—the issue is the congruence between what the mother *wants* to do and what she is doing. The benefits that are associated with maternal role satisfaction are both more optimal child functioning and more optimal parental functioning.

Unfortunately, the realities of being able to perform their preferred roles are not the same for all mothers. Many mothers do not want to be employed, yet their economic situation demands it. They then may be faced with finding child care, and they may not be eligible for public assistance programs. In some cases, mothers may be working unhappily in order to bring home a meager amount of money after taxes and child care are paid. These mothers would be better off if they were financially able to either stay at home or if they were able to find affordable child care. Mothers who are in this situation and believe that full-time parenting is more important than employment are struggling to resolve the internal conflict between the desire to stay at home and the need to be employed to make ends meet.

Policies to Increase Role Satisfaction

Because the research in the field has already shown the implications of dissatisfaction on both parenting and child development, it is clear that social policy needs to take this factor into
account. Policies and programs need to allow opportunities to
exist for both the mother who desires to work and the mother
who desires to stay at home.

The issue of role satisfaction poses slightly different conflicts
for the middle-income mother who can afford child care without
public assistance. These mothers can compete for better, more
satisfying jobs, or can financially choose to stay home if they
believe that full-time mothering is more important. In any event,
the children of these mothers will benefit if the mothers' attitudes
are congruent with their actual situations. Mothers in the middle-income level will typically have found child care they can
trust, thus reinforcing their beliefs that their children can do well
in their absence.

FLEXIBLE WORK ARRANGEMENTS

Sometimes the best choice for a woman who desires to combine
employment and family is to work part-time, especially when her
children are young and alternative care is expensive. Additionally, if she believes that full-time employment is not congruent
with attitudes about mothering, then her role satisfaction will be
more likely to be maintained if she can work part-time. Some
studies have also found that under certain conditions, women
who are employed part-time may enjoy closer mother/child
relationships, which can, in turn, enhance child development.

Part-time or flexible employment, however, is neither available
nor advantageous to all. Some variations of flexible work arrangements have been flextime, job sharing, permanent part-
time, telecommuting or home work, peak-time work, and voluntarily reduced work time. These variations all carry with them
differences in benefits, retirement plans, employment security,
and predictable incomes. Many part-time or flexible workers do

not enjoy any of these. This becomes an issue for single-parent women who need security as well as benefits. Many women who would rather work part-time are forced to join the full-time labor force in order to receive benefits for themselves and their children. For these women, full-time employment may decrease their satisfaction levels and parenting, thus affecting the development of their children.

In designing employment policy guidelines, elected officials can attend to these issues by focusing on the need for benefits to accompany flexible work arrangements. For example, job sharing can be set up so that two or more people can share a single job, salary, and a set of benefits. Flextime, part-time, or reduced work hours can involve the calculation of benefits that are proportionate with the amount of time worked without greatly increasing employer costs.

The temporary employment industry has become a growth industry. Many mothers of young children prefer it, and it can help to alleviate some financial and employment problems faced by some businesses in these troubled financial times. Public policy needs to recognize the issues that face the employed mother and try to work out solutions that benefit both employers and families.

A related issue that could be addressed by employers is that of the need for parents to monitor the after-school activities of older children. Research has indicated that when adolescent children of employed mothers are monitored while both parents are at work, they are less susceptible to antisocial peer pressure (Galambos & Maggs, 1991). Thus, it seems that the needs of employers, parents, and children could be addressed with policy decisions that incorporate these needs.

SUMMARY

A body of research is available that can direct and influence social policy decisions. The dynamics that connect maternal employment and child development are essential to the future health of individual families and the American society as a whole. The issues that researchers have been able to isolate have a day-to-day impact on the development of growing children and on the productivity of their employed mothers.

A multiplicity of dimensions come into play when thinking about the employed mother of today and her children. Social decision makers need to recognize the complexity because several policy sectors converge in any discussions of maternal employment and child development. A consensus needs to be achieved that crosses at least four categories of policy activity: social welfare policy, economic policy, employment policy, and early childhood education policy. Ultimately, what is needed is an approach that puts the families in the forefront and is responsive to the changes that confront them.

REVIEW QUESTIONS

1. Why do you think that policy programs that could help employed mothers have been few and far between? Do you think that policy-makers are influenced by their own views as to whether mothers should be employed?
2. Why are lower income families at an immense disadvantage for finding high-quality child care?
3. How can governmental policies help in providing after-school care and programs for elementary school children?
4. How do you think that flexible work policies might either benefit or hamper worker productivity?

SUGGESTED PROJECTS

1. Interview two employed mothers whom you know. Ask them what types of child care they use, if they are satisfied with them, and what led them to choose the particular types of care they use.
2. Interview three local businesses about their policies regarding flexible work arrangements. Ask them if they have any policies in place, and if not, why not. Try to get their perspectives on why they do or do not think such policies are useful.

References

Aberle, D. F., & Naegele, K. D. (1952). Middle-class fathers' occupational role and attitudes toward children. *American Journal of Orthopsychiatry, 22,* 366-378.

Ainsworth, M.D.S. (1973). The development of infant-mother attachment. In B. M. Caldwell & H. N. Ricciuti (Eds.), *Review of child development research* (Vol. 3, pp. 18-36). New York: Academic Press.

Ainsworth, M.D.S., Blehar, M. C., Waters, E., & Wall, S. (1978). *Patterns of attachment.* Hillsdale, NJ: Erlbaum.

Almquist, E. M. (1974). Sex stereotypes in occupational choice: The case for college women. *Journal of Vocational Behavior, 5,* 13-21.

Almquist, E. M., & Angrist, S. S. (1971). Role model influences on college women's career aspirations. *Merrill-Palmer Quarterly, 17,* 263-279.

Altman, S. L., & Grossman, F. K. (1977). Women's career plans and maternal employment. *Psychology of Women Quarterly, 1,* 365-376.

Alvarez, W. F. (1985). The meaning of maternal employment for mothers and their perceptions of their three-year old children. *Child Development, 56,* 350-360.

Anderson-Kulman, R. E., and Paludi, M.A. (1986). Working mothers and the family contest: Predicting positive coping. *Journal of Vocational Behavior, 28,* 241-253.

Astin, H. (1969). *The woman doctorate in America.* New York: Russell Sage.

Bacon, C., & Lerner, R. M. (1975). Effects of maternal employment status on the development of vocational-role perception in females. *Journal of Genetic Psychology, 126,* 187-193.

Baltes, P. B. (1979, Summer). On the potential and limits of child development: Life-span developmental perspectives. *Newsletter of the Society for Research in Child Development,* pp. 1-4.

Baltes, P. B., Reese, H. W., & Lipsitt, L. P. (1980). Life-span developmental psychology. *Annual Review of Psychology, 31,* 65-110.

Baltes, P. B., Reese, H. W., & Nesselroade, J. R. (1977). *Life-span developmental psychology: Introduction to research methods.* Monterey, CA: Brooks/Cole.

Banducci, R. (1967). The effect of mother's employment on the achievement, aspirations, and expectations of the child. *Personnel and Guidance Journal, 46,* 263-267.

Barling, J. (1986). Fathers' work experiences, the father-child relationship and children's behavior. *Journal of Occupational Behavior, 7,* 61-66.

Barling, J. (1990). Employment and marital functioning. In F. D. Fincham & T. Bardbury (Eds.), *The psychology of marriage: Conceptual, empirical, and applied perspectives* (pp. 201-225). New York: Praeger.

Barling, J. (1991). Father's employment: A neglected influence on children. In J. V. Lerner & N. L. Galambos (Eds.), *Employed mothers and their children* (pp. 181-209). New York: Garland.

Bartko, W. T., & Mc Hale, S. M. (1991). The household labor of children from dual-versus single-earner families. In J. V. Lerner & N. L. Galambos (Eds.), *Employed mothers and their children* (pp. 159-179). New York: Garland.

Baruch, G. K. (1972). Maternal influences upon college women's attitudes toward women and work. *Developmental Psychology, 6,* 32-37.

Beckman, K., Marsella, A. J., & Finney, R. (1979). Depression in the wives of nuclear submarine personnel. *American Journal of Psychiatry, 136,* 524-526.

Bell, R. Q. (1968). A reinterpretation of the direction of effects in studies of socialization. *Psychological Review, 75,* 81-95.

Below, H. I. (1972). *Life styles and roles of women as perceived by high-school girls.* Unpublished doctoral dissertation, Indiana University, Bloomington.

Belsky, J. (1984). Two waves of day care research: Developmental effects and conditions of quality. In R. Ainslie (Ed.), *The child and the day care setting* (pp. 1-34). New York: Praeger.

Belsky, J. (1986). Infant day care: A cause for concern? *Zero to Three, 6*(5), 1-9.

Belsky, J., & Rovine, M. J. (1988). Nonmaternal care in the first year of life and the security of infant-parent attachment. *Child Development, 59,* 157-176.

Blanchard, M., & Main, M. (1979). Avoidance of the attachment figure and social-emotional adjustment in day-care infants. *Developmental Psychology, 15,* 445-446.

Bowlby, J. (1951). *Maternal care and mental health.* Geneva: WHO; London: HMSO; New York: Columbia University Press.

Bowlby, J. (1969). *Attachment: Vol. 1. Attachment and loss.* New York: Basic Books.

Braverman, L. B. (1989). Beyond the myth of motherhood. In M. McGoldrick, C. M. Anderson, & F. Walsh (Eds.), *Women and families* (pp. 227-243). New York: Free Press.

Breakwell, G. M., Fife-Schaw, C., & Devereux, J. (1988). Parental influence and teenagers' motivation to train for technological jobs. *Journal of Occupational Psychology, 61,* 79-88.

Brim, O. G., Jr., & Kagan, J. (1980). Constancy and change: A view of the issues. In O. G. Brim, Jr., & J. Kagan (Eds.), *Constancy and change in human development* (pp. 1-25). Cambridge, MA: Harvard University Press.

Bronfenbrenner, U. (1988). Interacting systems in human development research paradigms: Present and future. In N. Bolger, A. Caspi, G. Downey, & M. Moorehouse (Eds.), *Persons in context: Developmental processes* (pp. 25-49). New York: Cambridge University Press.

Brofenbrenner, U., Alvarez, W. F., & Henderson, C. R. (1984). Working and watching: Maternal employment status and parents' perceptions of their three-year old children. *Child Development, 55,* 1362-1378.

Bronfenbrenner, U., & Crouter, A. C. (1982). Work and family through time and space. In S. B. Kamerman & C. D. Hayes (Eds.), *Families that work: Children in a changing world* (pp. 39-83). Washington, DC: National Academy Press.

Brooks-Gunn, J. (1989, November). *Opportunities for change: Effects of intervention programs on mothers and children.* Paper presented at the National Forum on Children and the Family Support Act, Washington, DC.

Brown, S. W. (1970). *A comparative study of maternal employment and non-employment.* Unpublished doctoral dissertation, Mississippi State University (University Microfilms 70-8610).

Burchinal, L. B. (1963). Personality characteristics of children. In F. I. Nye & L. W. Hoffman (Eds.), *The employed mother in America* (pp. 54-71). Chicago: Rand McNally.

Burchinal, M., Lee, M., & Ramey, C. (1989). Type of day-care and preschool intellectual development in disadvantaged children. *Child Development, 60,* 128-137.

Center for Human Resource Research. (1982). *The National Longitudinal Surveys Handbook.* College of Administrative Science, Ohio State University, Columbus.

Chandler, T. A., Sawicki, R. F., & Struffler, J. M. (1981). Relationship between adolescent sexual stereotypes and working mothers. *Journal of Early Adolescence, 1,* 72-83.

Chase-Lansdale, P. L., Michael, R. T., & Desai, S. (1991). Maternal employment during infancy: An analysis of "Children of the National Longitudinal Survey of Youth (NLSY)." In J. V. Lerner & N. L. Galambos (Eds.), *Employed mothers and their children* (pp. 37-61). New York: Garland.

Clark-Stewart, A. (1989). Infant day care: Malignant or maligned? *American Psychologist, 44,* 266-273.

Clark-Stewart, K. A., & Fein, G. (1983). Early childhood programs. In H. Haith & J. J. Campos (Eds.), *Infancy and developmental psychobiology* (Vol. 2, pp. 917-1000). New York: John Wiley.

Cotterell, J. L. (1986). Work and community influences on the quality of child rearing. *Child Development, 57,* 362-374.

Crouter, A. C. (1984). Spillover from family to work: The neglected side of the work-family interface, *Human Relations, 37,* 425-442.

Crouter, A. C., Belsky, J., & Spanier, G. B. (1984). The family context of child development: Divorce and maternal employment. In G. Whitehurst (Ed.), *The annuals of child development* (pp. 201-238). Greenwich, CT: JAI.

Crouter, A. C., & Garbarino, J. (1982). Corporate self-reliance and the sustainable society. *Technological Forecasting and Social Change, 22,* 139-151.

D'Amico, R. J., Haurin, R. J., & Mott, F. L. (1983). The effects of mothers' employment on adolescent and early adult outcomes of young men and women. In C. D. Hayes & S. B. Kamerman (Eds.), *Children of working parents: Experiences and outcomes* (pp. 130-219). Washington, DC: National Academy Press.

DeChick, J. (1988, July 19). Most mothers want a job, too. *USA Today,* p. D1.

Dellas, M., Gaier, E. L., & Emihovich, C. A. (1979). Maternal employment and selected behaviors and attitudes of preadolescents and adolescents. *Adolescence, 14,* 579-589.

Douvan, E. (1963). Employment and the adolescent. In F. I. Nye & L. W. Hoffman (Eds.), *The employed mother in America* (pp. 142-164). Chicago: Rand McNally.

Douvan, E., & Adelson, J. (1966). *The adolescent experience.* New York: John Wiley.

Duckett, E., & Richards, M. H. (1989, April). *Maternal employment and young adolescents' daily experience in single-mother families.* Paper presented at the Biennial Meeting of the Society for Research on Child Development, Kansas City, MO.

Elder, G. H., Jr. (1975). Age differentiation and the life course. *Annual Review of Sociology, 1,* 165-190.

Elder, G. H., Jr. (1981). History and the life course. In D. Bertaux (Ed.), *Biography and society: The life history approach in the social sciences* (pp. 77-115). Beverly Hills, CA: Sage.

Emmons, C., Biernat, M., Tiedje, L. B., Lang, E., & Wortman, C. (1990). Stress, support, and coping among women professionals with preschool children. In J. Eckenrode & S. Gore (Eds.), *Stress between work and family* (pp. 61-93). New York: Plenum.

Etaugh, C. (1980). Effects of nonmaternal care on children: Research evidence and popular views. *American Psychologist, 35,* 309-319.

Farber, E. A., & Egeland, B. (1982). Developmental consequences of out-of-home care for infants in a low income population. In E. Zigler & E. Gordon (Eds.), *Day care: Scientific and social policy issues* (pp. 102-125). Boston: Auburn.

Farel, A. M. (1980). Effects of preferred maternal roles, maternal employment, and sociographic status on school adjustment and competence. *Child Development, 50,* 1179-1186.

Featherman, D. L. (1983). Life-span perspectives in social science research. In P. B. Baltes & O. G. Brim, Jr. (Eds.), *Life-span development and behavior* (Vol. 5, pp. 1-57). New York: Academic Press.

Fox, M. F., & Hesse-Biber, S. (Eds.) (1984). *Women at work.* Mountain View, CA: Mayfield.

Frankel, E. (1964). Characteristics of working and non-working mothers among intellectually gifted high and low achievers. *Personnel and Guidance Journal, 42,* 776-780.

Furstenberg, F. F., Jr., Brooks-Gunn, J., & Chase-Lansdale, P. L. (1989). Teenaged pregnancy and childbearing. *American Psychologist, 44,* 313-320.

Galambos, N. L., & Maggs, J. L. (1991). Children in self-care: Figures, facts, and fiction. In J. V. Lerner and N. L. Galambos (Eds.), *Employed mothers and their children* (pp. 131-157). New York: Garland.

Galambos, N. L., Petersen, A. C., & Lenerz, K. (1988). Maternal employment and sex typing in early adolescence: Contemporaneous and longitudinal relations. In A. E. Gottfried & A. W. Gottfried (Eds.), *Maternal employment and children's development: Longitudinal research* (pp. 155-189). New York: Plenum.

Gilbert, L. A. (1985). *Men in dual-career families: Current realities and future prospects.* Hillsdale, NJ: Erlbaum.

Gilbert, L.A. (1988). *Sharing it all: The rewards and struggles of two-career families.* New York: Plenum.

Gilroy, F. D., Talierco, T. M., & Steinbacher, R. (1981). Impact of maternal employment on daughters' sex-role orientation and fear of success. *Psychological Reports, 49,* 963-968.

Gold, D., & Andres, D. (1977). Maternal employment and child development at three age levels. *Journal of Research and Development in Education, 10,* 20-29.

Gold, D., & Andres, D. (1978a). Relations between maternal employment and development of nursery school children. *Canadian Journal of Behavioral Science, 10*(2), 116-129.

Gold, D., & Andres, D. (1978b). Developmental comparisons between ten-year-old children with employed and nonemployed mothers. *Child Development, 49,* 75-84.

Goldberg, W. A., & Easterbrooks, M. A. (1988). Maternal employment when children are toddlers and kindergartners. In A. E. Gottfried & A. W. Gottfried

(Eds.), *Maternal employment and children's development: Longitudinal research* (pp. 121-154). New York: Plenum.

Golden, M., Rosenbluth, L., Grossi, M. T., Policare, H. J., Freeman, H., Jr., & Brownlee, E. M. (1978). *The New York City infant day care study*. New York: Medical and Health Research Association of New York City.

Gottfried, A. E. (1991). Maternal employment in the family setting: Developmental and environmental issues. In J. V. Lerner & N. L. Galambos (Eds.), *Employed mothers and their children* (pp. 63-84). New York: Garland.

Gottfried, A. E., & Gottfried, A. W. (1988). Maternal employment and children's development: An integration of longitudinal findings with implications for social policy. In A. E. Gottfried & A. W. Gottfried (Eds.), *Maternal employment and children's development: Longitudinal research* (pp. 269-287). New York: Plenum.

Gottfried, A. E., Gottfried, A. W., & Bathurst, K. (1988). Maternal employment, family environment, and children's development: Infancy through the school years. In A. E. Gottfried & A. W. Gottfried (Eds.), *Maternal employment and children's development: Longitudinal research* (pp. 11-58). New York: Plenum.

Greenberger, E., & O'Neil, R. (1992). Maternal employment and perceptions of young children: Bronfenbrenner et al. revisited. *Child Development, 63,* 431-448.

Grossman, F. K., Pollack, W. S., & Golding, E. (1988). Fathers and children: Predicting the quality and quantity of fathering. *Developmental Psychology, 24,* 82-91.

Hansson, R. O., Chernovetz, M. E., & Jones, W. H. (1977). Maternal employment and androgyny. *Psychology of Women Quarterly, 2,* 76-78.

Hetherington, E. M., Camara, K. A., & Featherman, D. L. (1983). Achievement and intellectual functioning of children in one-parent households. In J. Spence (Ed.), *Achievement and achievement motives* (pp. 205-284). San Francisco: Freeman.

Heyns, B., & Catsambis, S. (1986). Mother's employment and children's achievement: A critique. *Sociology of Education, 59,* 140-151.

Hillenbrand, E. D. (1976). Father absence in military families. *The Family Coordinator, 4,* 451-458.

Hochschild, A. (1989). *The second shift*. New York: Viking.

Hock, E. (1978). Working and non-working mothers with infants: Perceptions of their careers, their infants' needs, and satisfaction with mothering. *Developmental Psychology, 14,* 37-43.

Hock, E. (1980). Working and nonworking mothers and their infants: A comparative study of maternal caregiving characteristics and infant social behavior. *Merrill-Palmer Quarterly, 26,* 79-101.

Hofferth, S. L., & Phillips, D. H. (1987). Child care in the United States, 1970 to 1995. *Journal of Marriage and the Family, 49,* 559-571.

Hoffman, L. W. (1963). Mother's enjoyment of work and effects on the child. In F. I. Nye & L. W. Hoffman (Eds.), *The employed mother in America* (pp. 95-105). Westport, CT: Greenwood.

Hoffman, L. W. (1974). Effects of maternal employment on the child—A review of the research. *Developmental Psychology, 10,* 204-228.

Hoffman, L. W. (1979). Maternal employment: 1979. *American Psychologist, 34,* 859-865.

Hoffman, L. W. (1980). The effects of maternal employment on the academic attitudes and performance of school-aged children. *School Psychology Review, 9,* 319-335.

Hoffman, L. W. (1984). Maternal employment and the young child. In M. Perlmutter (Ed.), *Minnesota symposium in child psychology* (Vol. 17, pp. 101-127). Hillsdale, NJ: Erlbaum.

Hoffman, L. W. (1989). Effects of maternal employment in the two-parent family. *American Psychologist, 44,* 283-292.

Huston-Stein, A., & Higgins-Trenk, A. (1978). Development of females from childhood through adulthood: Career and feminine role orientations. In P. B. Baltes (Ed.), *Lifespan development and behavior* (Vol. 1, pp. 257-296). New York: Academic Press.

Hutner, F. C. (1972). Mother's education and working: Effect on the school child. *Journal of Psychology, 82,* 27-37.

Jensen, P. G., & Kirschner, W. K. (1955). A national answer to the question, "Do sons follow their fathers' occupations?" *Journal of Applied Psychology, 39,* 419-421.

Joebgen, A., & Richards, M. H. (1990). Maternal employment and education, maternal emotional adjustment, and adolescent emotional adjustment. *Journal of Early Adolescence, 10,* 329-343.

Jones, J. B., Lundsteen, S. W., & Michael, W. B. (1967). The relationship of the professional employment status of mother to reading achievement of sixth-grade children. *California Journal of Educational Research, 43,* 102-108.

Kagan, J. (1987). Perspectives on infancy. In J. Osofsky (Ed.), *Handbook of infant development* (2nd ed., pp. 1150 -1198). New York: John Wiley.

Kemper, T. D., & Reichler, M. L. (1976). Father's work integration and types and frequencies of rewards and punishments administered by fathers and mothers to adolescent sons and daughters. *Journal of Genetic Psychology, 129,* 207-219.

King, K., McIntyre, J., & Axelson, L. J. (1968). Adolescents' views of maternal employment as threat to the marital relationship. *Journal of Marriage and the Family, 30,* 633-637.

Klaus, M. H., & Kennell, J. H. (1976). *Maternal-infant bonding.* St. Louis, MO: Mosby.

Kohn, M. L. (1977). *Class & conformity.* Chicago: University of Chicago Press.

Lamb, M. E. (1981). The development of father-infant relationships. In M. E. Lamb (Ed.), *The role of the father in child development* (rev. ed.). New York: John Wiley.

Lamb, M. E. (1982). Parental influences on early socio-emotional development. *Journal of Child Psychology and Psychiatry, 23,* 185-190.

Lamb, M. E. (1988). Social and emotional development in infancy. In M. H. Bornstein & M. E. Lamb (Eds.), *Developmental psychology: An advanced textbook* (pp.359-410). Hillsdale, NJ: Erlbaum.

Lamb, M. E., & Campos, J. J. (1983). *Development in infancy: An introduction.* New York: Random House.

Lamb, M. E., Chase-Lansdale, P. L., & Owen, M. T. (1979). The changing American family and its implications for infant social development: The sample case of maternal employment. In M. Lewis & L. A. Rosenblum (Eds.), *The child and its family* (pp. 267-291). New York: Plenum.

Lamb, M. E., Frodi, A. M., Hwang, C. P., & Frodi, M. (1982). Varying degrees of paternal involvement in infant care: Attitudinal and behavioral correlates. In M. E. Lamb (Ed.), *Nontraditional families: Parenting and child development* (pp. 117-138). Hillsdale, NJ: Erlbaum.

Lamb, M. E., Thompson, R. A., Gardner, W. R., & Charnov, E. L. (1985). *Infant-mother attachment: The origins and developmental significance of individual differences in strange situation behavior.* Hillsdale, NJ: Erlbaum.

Lamb, M. E., Thompson, R. A., Gardner, W. R., Charnov, E. L., & Estes, D. P. (1984). Security of infantile attachment as assessed in the "strange situation": Its study and biological interpretation. *Behavioral and Brain Sciences, 7,* 121-171.

Larson, R. W., & Richards, M. H. (1991). Daily companionship in childhood and adolescence: Changing developmental contexts. *Child Development, 62,* 636-644.

Lazar, I., Darlington, R. B., Murray, H., Royce, J., & Snipper, A. (1982). Lasting effects of early education: A report from the Consortium for Longitudinal Studies. *Monographs of the Society of Research in Child Development, 47,* (Nos. 2-3, Serial No. 195).

Lerner, J. V., & Abrams, L. A. (in press). Developmental correlates of maternal employment influences on children. In C. Fisher & R. M. Lerner (Eds.), *Applied developmental psychology.* New York: McGraw-Hill.

Lerner, J. V., & Galambos, N. L. (1985). Maternal role satisfaction, mother-child interaction, and child temperament: A process model. *Developmental Psychology, 21,* 1157-1164.

Lerner, J. V., & Galambos, N. L. (1986). Child development and family change: The influences of maternal employment on infants and toddlers. In L. P. Lipsitt & C. Rovee-Collier (Eds.), *Advances in infancy research* (Vol. 4, pp. 39-86). Norwood, NJ: Ablex.

Lerner, J. V., & Galambos, N. L. (1988). The influences of maternal employment across life: The New York Longitudinal Study. In A. E. Gottfried & A. W. Gottfried (Eds.), *Maternal employment and children's development: Longitudinal research* (pp. 59-83). New York: Plenum.

Lerner, J. V., & Hess, L. E. (1988). Maternal employment influences on early adolescent development. In M. E. Levine & E. R. McArarney (Eds.), *Early adolescent transitions* (pp. 69-78). Lexington, MA: D. C. Heath.

Lerner, J. V., Hess, L. W., & Tubman, J. (1986, March). *Maternal employment, maternal role satisfaction, and early adolescent outcomes.* Paper presented at the First Meeting of the Society for Research in Adolescence, Madison, WI.

Lerner, R. M., & Busch-Rossnagel, N. A. (1981). Individuals as producers of their development: Conceptual and empirical bases. In R. M. Lerner & N. A. Busch-Rossnagel (Eds.), *Individuals as producers of their development: A life-span perspective* (pp. 1-36). New York: Academic Press.

Lerner, R. M., & Hultsch, D. F. (1983). *Human development: A life-span perspective.* New York: McGraw Hill.

Lerner, R. M., Hultsch, D. F., & Dixon, R. A. (1983). Contextualism and the character of developmental psychology in the 1970s. *Annuals of the New York Academy of Sciences, 412,* 101-128.

Lerner, R. M., Spanier, G. B., & Belsky, J. (1982). The child in the family. In C. B. Kopp & J. Krakow (Eds.), *The child: Development in a social context* (pp. 395-455). Reading, MA: Addison-Wesley.

Lorenz, K. Z. (1965). *Evolution and the modification of behavior.* Chicago: University of Chicago Press.

Lynn, D. B., & Sawrey, W. L. (1959). The effects of father-absence on Norwegian boys and girls. *Journal of Abnormal and Social Psychology, 59,* 258-262.

Marantz, S. A., & Mansfield, A. I. (1977). Maternal employment and the develop-
    ment of sex-role stereotyping in five-to-eleven-year-old girls. *Child Develop-
    ment, 48,* 668-673.
Mackinnon, C. E., Brody, G. H., & Stoneman, Z. (1982). The effects of divorce and
    maternal employment on the home environments of preschool children. *Child
    Development, 53,* 1392-1399.
Marsella, A. J., Dubanoski, R. A., & Mohs, K. (1974). The effects of father presence
    and absence upon maternal attitudes. *Journal of Genetic Psychology, 125,* 257-263.
McCartney, K., & Phillips, D. (1988). Motherhood and child care. In B. Birns & D.
    Haye (Eds.), *Different faces of motherhood* (pp. 157-183). New York: Plenum.
McCord, J., McCord, W., & Thurber, E. (1963). Effects of maternal employment
    on lower-class boys. *Journal of Abnormal and Social Psychology, 47,* 177-182.
McKinley, D. G. (1964). *Social class and family life.* New York: Free Press.
Meier, H. C. (1972). Mother-centeredness and college youths' attitudes toward
    social equality for women: Some empirical findings. *Journal of Marriage and the
    Family, 34,* 115-121.
Milne, A. M., Myers, D. E., Rosenthal, A. S., & Ginsburg, A. (1986). Single parents,
    working mothers, and the educational achievement of school children. *Sociol-
    ogy of Education, 59,* 125-139.
Montemayor, R. (1984). Maternal employment and adolescents' relations with
    parents, siblings and peers. *Journal of Youth and Adolescence, 13,* 543-557.
Montemayor, R., & Brownlee, J. R. (1982). *The mother-adolescent relationship in early
    and middle adolescence: Differences in maternal satisfaction.* Unpublished manu-
    script, University of Utah, Department of Family and Consumer Studies, Salt
    Lake City.
Montemayor, R., & Clayton, M. D. (1983). Maternal employment and adolescent
    development. *Theory Into Practice, 22,* 112-118.
Moorehouse, M. J. (1991). Linking maternal employment patterns to mother-
    child activities and children's school competence. *Developmental Psychology,
    27,* 295-303.
Mortimer, J. T. (1974). Patterns of intergenerational occupational movements: A
    small space analysis. *American Journal of Sociology, 79,* 1278-1299.
Mortimer, J. T. (1980). Occupation-family linkages as perceived by men in the
    early stages of professional and managerial careers. In Mortimer, J. T., *Research
    in the interweave of social roles: Vol. 1. Women and men* (pp. 99-117). Greenwich,
    CT: JAI.
Mortimer, J. T., Lorence, J., & Kumka, D. S. (1986). *Work, family, and personality:
    Transition to adulthood.* Norwood, NJ: Ablex.
Nelson, D. D. (1971). A study of personality adjustment among adolescent
    children with working and nonworking mothers. *Journal of Educational Re-
    search, 64,* 328-330.
Nelson, E. (1939). Father's occupation and student vocational choices. *School and
    Society, 50,* 572-576.
Nesselroade, J. R., & Baltes, P. B. (1974). Adolescent personality development and
    historical change: 1970-1972. *Monographs of the Society for Research in Child
    Development, 39,* (154).
Nesselroade, J. R., & Baltes, P. B. (1979). *Longitudinal research in the study of behavior
    and development.* New York: Academic Press.

O'Connell, M. & Bachu, A. (1988). Who's minding the kids? *Current Population Reprints*, pp. 70-30, U.S. Bureau of the Census.

Owen, M. T., Chase-Lansdale, L., & Lamb, M. E. (1984). *Mothers' and fathers' attitudes, maternal employment, and the security of infant-parent attachment*. Unpublished manuscript, University of Michigan, Ann Arbor.

Owen, M. T., & Cox, M. J. (1988). Maternal employment and the transition to parenthood. In A. E. Gottfried & A. W. Gottfried (Eds.), *Maternal employment and children's development: Longitudinal research* (pp. 85-119). New York: Plenum.

Pearlman, V. A. (1980). Influences of mothers' employment on career orientation and career choice of adolescent daughters. *Dissertation Abstracts International, 41*(11-A), 4657-4658.

Pedersen, F. A., Cain, R. A., Zaslow, M. J., & Anderson, B. J. (1982). Variation in infant experience associated with alternative family roles. In L. Loasa and I. Sigel (Eds.), *Families as learning environments for children* (pp. 203-221). New York: Plenum.

Phillips, D., McCartney, K., Scarr, S., & Howes, C. (1987). Selective review of infant day care research: A cause for concern! *Zero to Three, 7*(1), 18-21.

Piotrkowski, C. (1979). *Work and the family system*. New York: Free Press.

Piotrkowski, C. S., & Gornick, L. K. (1987). Effects of work-related separations on children and families. In C. S. Piotrkowski & L. K. Gornick, *The psychology of work and loss* (pp. 267-299). San Francisco: Jossey-Bass.

Piotrkowski, C. S., & Stark, E. (1987). Children and adolescents look at their parents' jobs. In J. H. Lewko (Ed.), *How children and adolescents view the world of work* (pp. 3-19). San Francisco: Jossey-Bass.

Pistrang, N. (1984). Women's work involvement and experience of new motherhood. *Journal of Marriage and the Family, 46*, 433-447.

Place, T. (1987). *A report on corporate involvement in child care*. Westport, CT: Developmental Child Care, Inc.

Pleck, J. H. (1985). *Working wives/Working husbands*. Beverly Hills, CA: Sage.

Powell, K. (1963). Personalities of children and child-rearing attitudes of mothers. In F. I. Nye & L. W. Hoffman (Eds.), *The employed mother in America* (pp. 125-141). Chicago: Rand McNally.

Query, J. M., & Kuruvilla, T. C. (1975). Male and female adolescent achievement and maternal employment. *Adolescence, 10*, 353-356.

Ramey, C. T., & Campbell, F. (1987). The Carolina Abecedarian Project: An educational experiment concerning human malleability. In J. J. Gallagher & C. T. Ramey (Eds.), *The malleability of children* (pp. 127-139). Baltimore: Brooks.

Rees, A. N., & Palmer, G. H. (1970). Factors related to change in mental test performance. *Developmental Psychology Monograph, 3*, (2, Pt. 2).

Richards, M. H., & Duckett, E. (1991). Maternal employment and adolescents. In J. V. Lerner & N. L. Galambos (Eds.), *Employed mothers and their children* (pp. 98-130). New York: Garland.

Richardson, J. L., Dwyer, K., McGuigan, K., Hanson, W. B., Dent, C., Johnson, C. A., Sussman, S. Y., Brannon, B., & Flay, B. (1989). Substance use among eighth grade students who take care of themselves after school. *Pediatrics, 84*, 556-566.

Rosenthal, D., & Hansen, J. (1981). The impact of maternal employment on children's perceptions of parents and personal development. *Sex Roles, 1*, 593-598.

Roy, P. (1963). Adolescent roles: Rural-urban differentials. In F. I. Nye & L. W. Hoffman (Eds.), *The employed mother in America* (pp. 165-181). Chicago: Rand McNally.

Santrock, J. W. (Ed.) (1989). *Life-span development* (3rd ed.). Dubuque, IA: William C. Brown.

Sattler, J. M. (1974). *Assessment of children's intelligence.* Philadelphia: Saunders.

Scarr, S. (1984). *Mother care, other care.* New York: Basic Books.

Scarr, S., Phillips, D., & McCartney, K. (1989). Dilemmas of child care in the United States: Employed mothers and children at risk. *Canadian Psychology/Psychologie Canadienne, 30,* 126-138.

Schacter, F. F. (1981). Toddlers with employed mothers. *Child Development, 59,* 958-964.

Schroeder, P. (1988). Family & medical leave part I. In F. E. Winfield (Ed.), *The work and family source-book.* Greenvale, NY: Panel Publications.

Schwartz, J. C., Scarr, S. W., Caparulo, B., Furrow, D., McCartney, K., Billington, R., Phillips, D., & Hindy, C. (1981, August). *Center, sitter, and home day care before age two. A report on the first Bermuda infant care study.* Paper presented at the annual meeting of the American Psychological Association, Los Angeles, CA.

Silverstein, L. B. (1991). Transforming the debate about child care and maternal employment. *American Psychologist, 46,* 1025-1032.

Smith, H. G. (1969). *An investigation of the attitudes of adolescent girls toward combining marriage, motherhood, and a career.* Unpublished doctoral dissertation, Columbia University, New York. (University microfilms 69-8089).

Spitz, R. (1946). Anaclitic depression. *Psychoanalytic Study of the Child, 2,* 313-342.

Stein, A. H. (1973). The effects of maternal employment and educational attainment on the sex-typed attributes of college females. *Social Behavior and Personality, 1,* 111-114.

Steinberg, L. (1986). Latchkey children and susceptibility to peer pressure: An ecological analysis. *Developmental Psychology, 22,* 433-439.

Stuckey, M. F., McGhee, P. E., & Bell, N. J. (1982). Parent-child interaction: The influence of maternal employment. *Developmental Psychology, 18,* 635-644.

Svejda, M., Campos, J., & Emde, R. N. (1980). Mother-infant "bonding": Failure to generalize. *Child Development, 51,* 775-779.

Tangri, S. S. (1972). Determinants of occupational role innovation among college women. *Journal of Social Issues, 28,* 177-199.

Thompson, R. A. (1991). Infant day care: Concerns, controversies, choices. In J. V. Lerner & N. L. Galambos (Eds.), *Employed mothers and their children* (pp. 9-36). New York: Garland.

Thompson, R. A., & Lamb, M. E. (1986). Infant-mother attachment: New directions for theory and research. In P. B. Baltes, D. L. Featherman, & R. M. Lerner (Eds.), *Life-span development and behavior* (Vol. 7, pp. 1-41). Hillsdale, NJ: Erlbaum.

Trimberger, R., & MacLean, M. J. (1982). Maternal employment: The child's perspective. *Journal of Marriage and the Family, 44,* 469-475.

U.S. Bureau of Census. (1987). *After-school care of school-age children: December 1984* (Current Population Reports, Series P-23, No. 149). Washington, DC: Government Printing Office.

U.S. Bureau of Census. (1991). *Current population reports* (Series P-20, No. 454). Washington, DC: Government Printing Office.

U.S. Department of Health and Human Services. (1991). Child Care and Developmental Block Grant. *Federal Register*, Vol. 56, No. 109, 26194. Washington, DC.

U.S. Bureau of Labor Statistics. (1991). *Bulletin 2340*. Washington, DC: Government Printing Office.

VanFossen, B. E. (1977). Sexual stratification and sex-role socialization. *Journal of Marriage and the Family, 39*, 563-574.

Vogel, S. R., Broverman, I. K., Broverman, D. M., Clarkson, F. E., & Rosenkrantz, P. S. (1970). Maternal employment and perception of sex roles among college students. *Developmental Psychology, 3*, 384-391.

Voydanoff, P. (1982). Work roles and quality of family life among professionals and managers. In B. M. Hirschlein and W. J. Braun (Eds.), *Families and work* (pp. 118-124). Stillwater: Oklahoma State University Press.

Voydanoff, P., & Kelly, R. F. (1984). Determinants of work-related family problems among employed parents. *Journal of Marriage and the Family, 46*, 881-892.

Warr, P., & Parry, G. (1982). Paid employment and women's psychological well-being. *Psychological Bulletin, 91*, 498-516.

Werts, G. E. (1968). Paternal influence on career choice. *Journal of Counseling Psychology, 15*, 48-52.

Williamson, S. Z. (1970). The effects of maternal employment on the scholastic performance of children. *Journal of Home Economics, 62*, 609-613.

Wortman, C. (1987, October). Coping with role overload among professionals with young children. In K. P. Matthews (Chair), *Workshop on Women, Work, and Health*. Workshop conducted at the meeting of the MacArthur Foundation, Hilton Head, SC.

Woods, M. B. (1972). The unsupervised child of the working mother. *Developmental Psychology, 6*, 14-25.

Yarrow, M. R., Scott, P., deLeeuw, L., & Heinig, C. (1962). Child-rearing in families of working and nonworking mothers. *Sociometry, 25*, 122-140.

Zaslow, M. J. (1987). *Sex differences in children's response to maternal employment*. Unpublished manuscript, prepared for the Committee on Child Development Research and Public Policy, National Research Council, Washington, D.C.

Zaslow, M. J., & Hayes, C. D. (1986). Sex differences in children's response to psychosocial stress: Toward a cross-context analysis. In M. E. Lamb, A. Brown, & B. Rogoff (Eds.), *Advances in developmental psychology* (Vol. 4, pp. 287-335). Hillsdale, NJ: Erlbaum.

Zaslow, M. J., Pedersen, F., Suwalsky, J., Cain, R., Anderson, B., & Fival, M. (1985). The early resumption of employment by mothers: Implications for parent-infant interaction. *Journal of Applied Developmental Psychology, 6*, 1-16.

Zaslow, M. J., Rabinovich, B. A., & Suwalsky, J.T.D. (1991). From maternal employment to child outcomes: Preexisting group differences and moderating variables. In J. V. Lerner & N. L. Galambos (Eds.), *Employed mothers and their children* (pp. 237-282). New York: Garland.

Author Index

Subject Index

About the Author

Jacqueline V. Lerner is Professor of Psychology at Michigan State University. She received a bachelor's degree in psychology from St. John's University, a master's degree in psychology from Eastern Michigan University, and a doctoral degree in educational psychology from Pennsylvania State University. She has coedited *Temperament and Psychosocial Interaction in Infancy and Childhood* and *Employed Mothers and Their Children*. Her research on the influences of maternal employment on child development and temperamental contributions to development has been published in numerous scholarly journals.